TO THE LAST BITE

RECIPES AND IDEAS
FOR MAKING THE MOST OF
YOUR INGREDIENTS

ALEXIS deBOSCHNEK

SIMON & SCHUSTER

NEW YORK   LONDON   TORONTO   SYDNEY   NEW DELHI

Simon & Schuster
1230 Avenue of the Americas
New York, NY 10020

First Simon & Schuster hardcover edition April 2022

SIMON & SCHUSTER and colophon are registered trademarks of Simon & Schuster, Inc.

For information about special discounts for bulk purchases, please contact Simon & Schuster Special Sales at 1-866-506-1949 or business@simonandschuster.com.

The Simon & Schuster Speakers Bureau can bring authors to your live event. For more information or to book an event, contact the Simon & Schuster Speakers Bureau at 1-866-248-3049 or visit our website at www.simonspeakers.com.

Interior design by Ruth Lee-Mui

Manufactured in China

1   3   5   7   9   10   8   6   4   2

Library of Congress Cataloging-in-Publication Data has been applied for.

ISBN 978-1-9821-5138-6
ISBN 978-1-9821-5143-0 (ebook)

For my mother, my greatest inspiration,
for this book and in my life

CONTENTS

INTRODUCTION

Just three hours north of New York City stretches the bucolic region called the Catskill Mountains. Despite the area's rocky, unforgiving soil and relentless winters, the rolling hills are dotted with livestock and sprawling farms. The land is special to the farmers who have tended it for generations. In summer, it's green as far as the eye can see. Produce stands pop up on the edge of every dirt road, baskets overflowing with golden corn, crunchy snap peas straight off the vine, and every variety of tomato you can imagine. My family moved here when I was two, and to me, it's home.

The land became special to us, too. My mom is a master gardener, one of those people who can resurrect any plant from the edge of death as she rattles off its genus and species in Latin. So I spent my summers tagging along with her to gardens all over the county, absorbing as much as I could. She would point out what was a weed and what wasn't, show me how to spot an aphid (and, more important, how to get rid of those pesky insects), and taught me the precise moment vegetables were ripe for picking. I will always think of her pulling a carrot from the soil. "Now *this* is a real carrot!" she would say. And later: "*This* is how it should taste!"

My mother knew, and taught me, to make what we had sourced locally as the centerpiece of our meals. Sometimes this meant just-caught rainbow trout from the Delaware River stuffed with herbs from the garden. Other times it meant a mushroom tart in a flaky pastry with chanterelles she found in a nearby pine forest. One Thanksgiving I was given the painstaking task of carving out twenty miniature white pumpkins that she grew. We made creamy pumpkin soup and served it in the hollowed-out pumpkins. She packed me dizzyingly delicious school lunches: sandwiches layered with zucchini roasted with whole cloves of garlic, smothered in herby goat cheese, ribbons of prosciutto tucked into baguettes with fresh-made butter.

But these efforts were not simply about gardening and cooking. My mother also tried to waste as little as possible. Shrimp shells were saved for stock that would eventually go into Icelandic fish stew. Whatever food scraps we couldn't make good use of were reserved for our chickens so they, too, could eat well and lay eggs with the brightest orange yolks I've ever seen. Eggshells were put into the compost, and come spring, we would work what had been composted back into the garden's soil. We would then plant seeds in that soil to grow our produce for the year. Summer produce was canned and frozen to last until the following season. Everything had a purpose beyond its first use.

This dedication to the land extended well into my community. In high school, I finagled my way out of chemistry and instead took landscape and horticulture, where I learned to tap trees for maple syrup, use a chainsaw, design gardens, and grow my own tomato plants. As soon as the ice began to thaw in spring, my gym teacher would coax us into the Delaware River to teach us how to fly-fish. Class field trips were to the local beekeeper and nearby reservoirs.

We didn't talk about sustainability or regenerative agriculture—it was just the way things were done.

It wasn't until I left home that I heard those words. Throughout my twenties, I worked in restaurants and at a variety of food media jobs, doing everything from writing and interviewing chefs and developing recipes to merchandising for an online local grocery store. As sustainability became increasingly important, everywhere I worked made efforts to adapt. Despite their best attempts, there was still a staggering amount of waste. I'm not talking about some carrot tops being thrown away (although I think you should save those, too!), but bags of trash filled with food scraps. There are estimates that somewhere between 30 percent to 40 percent of the food produced in the United States is wasted, which translates to billions of pounds of food that ends up in landfills. All this wasted food produces methane, which contributes to global warming. Not only that, but food waste has a whole other slew of adverse effects, like taking a toll on the entire supply chain in terms of generating pollution, overusing clean water, and overworking the land. It's expensive in many ways for both us and the planet.

I thought that some of the things I had learned from my mother and my community might be helpful. Of course, my little pocket in upstate New York isn't the first or only place to practice this kind of sustainability. So many other communities—and countries—have been implementing their own methods for centuries. I wanted to share ideas like taking a few minutes of my day to compost vegetables, recycling whenever possible, using plastic wrap only when necessary, and sticking to a grocery list rather than impulse buying. These small steps may not feel groundbreaking, but they make a difference. I began to write a book that embodied this approach to food, encouraging others to cook more mindfully in a way that doesn't feel like a chore. I created recipes that called for a handful of good ingredients, listed methods that would make them shine, and offered ways to reduce waste.

And then the COVID-19 pandemic struck, changing our lives. Suddenly people were spending more time at home and cooking more meals than ever before. Friends who had lived off takeout were reaching out asking for accessible recipes for delicious food that could be prepared from a handful of good ingredients. Going to the grocery store multiple times a week just to pick up a few things was out of the question; they needed to cook with what they had on hand and needed to find ways to make that last. I sent many of the recipes included here to my friends.

There are hundreds of ideas out there for how to use scraps, but they're not all equally convenient—or frankly, delicious. Sure, you *can* save ginger peels to make tea with, but I never remember to do that. I don't know about you, but I'm never going to save a Halloween jack-o'-lantern to make pumpkin puree. This book is filled with recipes I cook weekly, like a potato and leek top (yes, leek tops!) frittata that feels kind of like eating sour cream and onion chips for breakfast, or the Greens Skillet Pie (page 83) that is sure to use up every green and herb in your fridge. Most of the recipes are vegetable focused, with meat and fish being reserved for special occasions rather than everyday.

I'm not against eating meat and fish—I love them—but I'm aware of the impact their production has on the environment. Most fish found at the grocery store comes from overfished waters, or farms that use antibiotics to combat the inevitable diseases brought on by overcrowding. The same goes for a lot of meat found at the grocery store, especially beef and pork, which comes from factory farms. It's not just about the animals, but about the people who are working for low wages at these jobs, the effects these practices have on the soil and our water, and the strain it puts on the food chain. I try to buy local, humanely raised meat and fish whenever possible, or at least sustainably raised if that's not an option. I know that's not always possible for everyone. The food system in the United States has created an inequitable system where buying the best food means paying a premium, one that many can't afford. That's why I wanted to create recipes that celebrate vegetables you can find at most grocery stores. You don't have to stop eating meat and fish, and I haven't, but I hope this book will encourage you to start eating more vegetables and save those proteins for more special occasions.

I've learned so much not only from my mom, but from Wendell Berry, Alice Waters, and Michael Pollan about food systems and how to think—and eat—more consciously. I'm far from being an expert or a model of perfection and have so much to learn still when it comes to practicing sustainability in my day-to-day life. I hope these recipes serve as a source of inspiration to start cooking more thoughtfully and resourcefully, down to the last bite.

HOW TO USE THIS BOOK

There are two ways you can use this book. The first is to use it like any other cookbook. Flip through the recipes to find one you want to make and head to the kitchen. Recipes are organized by traditional categories so you can decide what you want to make.

The second is more like those Choose Your Own Adventure books. Remember the books where you got to be the protagonist and chose how the action unfolded? Every recipe here leads to another recipe, and in most cases, to more than one. Start with one ingredient—your protagonist—then choose what comes next. The goal is to lead you to a satisfying end and down to the last bite—in this case, that's the bottom of that container of sour cream, or that final stem of parsley. There are recipes for showstopping dinners worth running to the store for, but plenty of other meals for the rest of the week to make with what you've already bought. At the end of each recipe, I list other recipes in this book that call for the ingredients you'll have left over when you finish your first dish.

Before I started writing this book, I polled a group of friends ranging from novice home cooks to professional chefs to learn what ingredients often went to waste. Regardless of their cooking ability, the answers were remarkably consistent. People buy big-ticket proteins with a particular recipe in mind, but vegetables, tender herbs, and dairy often get left to rot or spoil, so I wrote recipes to use them up.

I also wanted to highlight some parts of vegetables that get tossed, which often have just as much flavor. Fennel stalks are completely edible, yet they're often left for the compost. The same goes for the dark green leek tops, which, when cooked down with a good pat of butter, become downright silky. Parsley and cilantro stems are more intensely flavored than the leaves and add a welcome crunch to just about any dish. And once you've tried a roasted radish top—so salty and crunchy it tastes like a kettle chip—I hope you'll reconsider how you look at all ingredients.

You might notice as you read through the book that a lot of the ingredients are repeated, and that's intentional. Most ingredients can be bought at your grocery store, and anything that requires a specialty store or ordering online is used multiple times here.

However you choose to use this book, I hope that you will feel a renewed sense of excitement when you look in your fridge or go to the store. Not only will you be equipped with a set of foolproof recipes to use these ingredients, you'll also have ideas for how to use them in new ways.

PANTRY STAPLES

The pantry is broken up into two sections: shelf stable and perishable items. For shelf stable items—like canned tomatoes, capers, or cinnamon sticks—the idea is that you can simply gather them from your pantry before cooking. For perishable items—like produce and dairy, or ingredients that expire or are often tossed—I've focused on weaving the recipes together through the headnotes. This is not an exhaustive list of every pantry staple you could have. But these are the staples that I use most often in this book, and if you have them, you can make most of these recipes without having to do too much extra shopping.

SHELF STABLE STAPLES

Salt

I call for two types of salt in this book: kosher salt and flaky sea salt. Kosher salt is iodine-free (unlike table salt) and has coarser crystals, making it ideal for seasoning with ease. I—and most major food publications—recommend buying Diamond Crystal kosher brand, which is what I used to develop these recipes. If you use Morton's kosher salt, which is denser, make sure to halve the amount called for or you run the risk of having a supersalty dish.

I'm fairly obsessive about flaky sea salt, and finish nearly everything with it, savory and sweet alike. Maldon is the most widely available choice, but if you're looking to buy something American-made (well, harvested), check out Jacobsen Salt Co.

Oil

There are a few types of oil you should have. I keep a big jug of good olive oil (California Olive Ranch is my go-to) on hand for everyday cooking, as well as a slightly more expensive olive oil, like Brightland, available for things like vinaigrettes and aiolis where you're really going to taste the difference. Don't bother using the pricy stuff for preparations where the oil is going to disappear into the dish.

You also need a neutral oil with a high smoke point, which means the oil won't burn when the heat is turned up. I like grapeseed oil for its clean taste.

Once you have the basics, you can expand. I keep canola oil for when I want to deep-fry. Sesame oil adds nuttiness, and coconut oil imparts an almost tropical, fruity flavor.

Acid

There are two easy ways to add acid: citrus and vinegar.

The reason people talk about the importance of acid is because it simultaneously brightens and balances food. I've always made it a point to stock a handful of lemons and limes, but when I lived in Los Angeles, I learned there's so much more to taste when it comes to citrus. One apartment I lived in had a key lime tree in the front yard; another had a Meyer lemon tree. If you see any exciting citrus—blood oranges, pomelos, finger limes—buy them! You can use them in a California Citrus Salad (page 55), make a more adventurous flavored Orange Meringue Semifreddo (page 189), or swap in different citrus in vinaigrettes. Whenever I call for lemons in the ingredient list, the assumption is that the lemon should provide two tablespoons of juice. If you're using the zest, too, make sure to buy organic. While citrus is technically perishable, they're used so often that I didn't include them in the headnotes.

I hoard vinegar—I've always got champagne, sherry, balsamic, apple cider, rice, and white distilled vinegar on hand. Like citrus, vinegar adds acid, which helps balance the flavor of almost all savory preparations. If you're just getting started stocking your pantry, buy two or three of your favorites.

Mustard

Mustard gets its own shout-out for being so adaptable. Sure, it can be used as a classic condiment, slathered on hot dogs and burgers, but I also keep mustard on hand for vinaigrettes, marinades, and rubs. The overall effect rarely tastes of mustard, but without it you're missing a certain tanginess. While you could fill a whole fridge shelf with all the types of mustard, I'd recommend keeping a classic, smooth Dijon and as well as whole grain for some varied texture. You can really taste the difference in quality between mustards, so it's worth investing in the good stuff here. I like the French brand Maille.

Condiments

Who doesn't have a shelf full of condiments in their fridge? I'm constantly trying different hot sauces and spreads to add a boost of flavor to a dish. That said, these are my go-to, tried-and-true condiments that I always have on hand (and you should, too): ketchup, mayonnaise, at least one type of hot sauce, soy sauce, and fish sauce.

Something Briny

Olives, capers, and pickles make up my trifecta of briny must-haves. A four-ounce jar of capers takes up so little room in the refrigerator, and olives last for months. Bonus: they're great to add to a last-minute cheese spread.

Spices

No matter how many spices I have on hand, I tend to gravitate to the same handful. They are all readily available. If a recipe calls for a spice that you don't like, swap it with something similar that you do like. Store spices in sealable glass jars, out of sunlight and away from the stove, to keep them fresher longer. Most spices can keep for up to a year, but after that their flavor starts to become more muted. Keeping a smaller selection of spices you use more often is a great way to cut down on waste. Here are all the spices I use throughout the book: black peppercorns, coriander seeds, ground coriander, dried bay leaves, crushed red pepper flakes, paprika, smoked paprika, ground sumac, curry powder, ground cumin, ground cardamom, cayenne pepper, dried oregano, and ground cinnamon.

Canned Goods

Canned goods are the backbone of a well-stocked pantry. While I love the process of cooking dried beans, canned beans go far in a pinch, like in my Tuna and White Bean Salad (page 175). The same goes for canned tomatoes and tomato paste, which can add richness to a variety of dishes, like Red Wine Braised Short Rib Ragout (page 137) or Saucy Tomatoes and Eggs (page 217). I also keep canned fish like tuna, anchovies, and sardines on hand for quick meals when I want something light without a lot of effort. Anchovies are a not-so-secret weapon for adding a little hit of umami. Since they often come in cans, I've included recipes in the headnote for how to use them up.

On the Sweet Side

If you have any interest in baking or in sweets in general, I'd recommend keeping your pantry well stocked with sweeteners. I keep standard granulated sugar, light brown sugar, powdered sugar, and turbinado sugar (raw, coarse sugar) on hand. Unlike other ingredients in this book, they really can't be used interchangeably, and all serve their own purpose. I also stock honey and maple syrup, which I use in baked goods and breakfasts, as well as in savory preparations, like punchy vinaigrettes that

need to take the acid down a notch. Both have long shelf lives (honey never expires), so even if you don't use them weekly, have no fear about being wasteful.

Wine

I'm a huge proponent of cooking with wine and always keep red and white stocked. I use it for deglazing, braising, adding acid to a variety of dishes, and helping deepen flavor. A good rule of thumb is to use wine for cooking that you would want to drink since that's the flavor you're imparting onto the dish. The alcohol burns off during the cooking process, so you don't have to worry about your food tasting boozy. If you're abstaining from alcohol altogether, you can use stock (chicken or vegetable) whenever a recipe calls for wine. If you're not enjoying the rest of the bottle, store wine in the refrigerator after opening—white wine will last for months (for cooking, not drinking), and red wine can be used for up to five days.

PERISHABLE STAPLES

Herbs

I'm of the belief that a handful of herbs makes pretty much every dish taste better. There are two types of herbs: tender and hardy. As the name suggests, tender herbs have delicate stems and light, leafy bushels, like parsley, cilantro, basil, and dill. Hardy herbs have a woody stem, like rosemary, thyme, and sage. It's not sustainable to buy every type of herb every time you go shopping, but I like to buy at least one bunch of tender herbs and one bunch of hardy herbs at the beginning of the week, and add them to whatever I'm making as they're fairly interchangeable. If you're ever stuck on how to use them up, try a punchy salsa verde, which is my go-to. For parsley and cilantro, I've written the recipes here with the assumption that one bunch is equal to two cups. For any recipes that only use half a bunch or less, I've included other recipes in where you can use it up. For other herbs, the sizes vary too greatly depending on where you're buying them to include the bunch in the ingredient list.

Alliums

There's not much that alliums don't help enhance. Sautéed, caramelized, pickled, and raw, their fragrant, garlicky flavor adds a distinct depth. Keep alliums stored in a cool, dark place and they'll last weeks—if not months—making it worth your while to stock a full lineup of garlic, shallots, and both yellow and red onions. Leeks, scallions, and chives should be wrapped loosely in plastic and stored in the refrigerator to preserve freshness.

In addition to all the regular alliums, I also keep black garlic in the refrigerator. Black garlic is aged until it's got a black, almost lacquered look, with a sweet, umami flavor. It's worth seeking out. You can find black garlic at specialty grocery stores or do what I do and order it online. Since it's been cured, there's no real expiration date, making it an ideal pantry staple.

Dairy

I keep salted butter at room temperature to slather on toast, and unsalted butter in the refrigerator for everything else. I always keep a few sticks of butter in the freezer, which extends the shelf life by a few months and ensures that you'll never be faced with the dreaded realization that you'll have to wait until later to bake those cookies.

There's always at least one container of sour cream, yogurt, crème fraîche, or labneh (a type of thick, strained yogurt with a consistency close to cream cheese) floating around my fridge. They can almost always be used as substitutes for each other, with only minor changes to a recipe. All add a creaminess and tang to a variety of dishes. Save yogurt for Yogurt Chive Flatbread (page 37), a dollop of crème fraîche for porridge, or sour cream for Marbled Sour Cream Coffee Cake (page 200).

I keep at least one pint of heavy cream on hand for making an impromptu batch of whipped cream, thinning out buttercream frosting, making an egg wash for a pie, swirling into soup, or making caramel. Even once opened, heavy cream has a long shelf life, making it unlikely to go to waste.

Think about stocking cheese the way you would approach a cheese board. It's good to have something aged, something smooth, and something creamy. I always have a block of Parmigiano-Reggiano tucked away in my cheese drawer. Parmesan lasts forever and adds that umami flavor of earthy saltiness. Save the rinds in a bag and fish them out whenever you're ready to make stock or a stew. As a note, whenever I call for Parmesan, I'm referring to Parmigano-Reggiano. Apart from Parmesan, I always keep a few cheeses on hand, from nutty Gruyère, a sharp block of cheddar, and a salty ricotta salata, to a silky ball of burrata.

Eggs

I go through a staggering number of eggs every week. While they're technically perishable, I don't include whole eggs in the headnotes because I assume most people, like me, like having eggs on hand to fry, scramble, and poach. However, I do include recipes for how to use up extra yolks or whites. It always feels like a shame to waste them, and there are so many options to use them. Egg whites and yolks can stay fresh in a sealed container in the refrigerator for up to two days. I used large eggs throughout, and you should, too, in order to maintain accuracy when making these recipes.

Bread

I talk about bread a lot in this book. I don't mean for sandwiches, although obviously I use bread for that reason, but for all the other things you can do with it. I keep bread on hand for making crunchy croutons for soup, crispy pieces for panzanella (page 51), sopping up the broth of chorizo-spiked clams, and for making my own bread crumbs (panko works here in a pinch). I tend to favor a sourdough loaf with a good crust and tender crumb, but it's up to personal preference.

Nuts

You might notice in these pages that I've got a bit of a walnut obsession. I love the hearty texture they add, and, bonus, they're on the more affordable side of the nut spectrum. That said, keep a selection of your favorite nuts on hand. I store nuts in glass jars in the refrigerator to keep them fresher longer.

Ginger

A little bit of ginger goes a long way. I use ginger to add a sweet, peppery flavor to everything from earthy Farro with Mushrooms (page 123) and Curried Mussels with Basil (page 166) to a summertime Stone Fruit Crisp (page 179). Store it in the refrigerator for up to one month, or until it's become too shriveled to use. Pro tip: you don't have to peel ginger before using it, but if you want to, use the tip of a spoon to scrape the skin off the ginger. It'll come off in seconds.

KITCHEN TOOLS

I feel the same way about kitchen equipment that I do about ingredients: you can do a lot with a handful of good ones. Single-use tools have no place in my kitchen, nor do clunky gadgets that take up too much room. I promise I'll never ask you to go out and buy an avocado slicer (that's what a paring knife is for), olive pitter (the back of your knife works just as well), or one of those tools to remove kale stems (use your hands). A few times I call for using plastic wrap. I try to avoid single-use plastic as much as possible, but I haven't found a good alternative for things like wrapping pie dough in. If you have a better solution, please let me know!

I haven't listed every single tool here—there's some I hope you already have stocked, like a wooden spoon, colander, whisk, cutting board, and pot. Here are the tools I use regularly that you might not have and I think are worth investing in:

Chef's Knife

A chef's knife is the true workhorse of the kitchen, and I use it for everything from slicing and dicing to smashing and mincing. Find one with some weight to it. Look to see if the metal of the blade is visible all the way to the end of the handle—it's a good indication of quality. You should have one that feels comfortable in your hand, not so big that it feels like you're wielding a sword, and not so small that it feels like a steak knife. I think a ten-inch knife is a good place to start.

Rasp Grater

I use my rasp grater nearly daily. Use it for zesting citrus and grating cheese and fresh ginger. If you don't feel like mincing garlic, a rasp grater is a great shortcut. When I call for grating garlic, that's the time to whip out a rasp grater. My go-to brand is Microplane.

Fish Spatula

Don't let the name fool you: fish spatulas are remarkably versatile. They're more flexible than a standard spatula, and therefore arguably easier to use for just about everything. Use it to fry eggs, turn vegetables over, smash down burgers, lift cookies from a baking sheet, and of course, flip fish.

Vegetable Peeler

A basic Y-shaped vegetable peeler will take you far. It's not just for cleaning up root vegetables; you can also create delicate ribbons, like for the Carrot Ribbon Salad (page 59), or for peeling rinds of citrus to candy.

Dutch Oven

It's worth it to splurge on a big Dutch oven. It'll last a lifetime, and you can use it for everything from braising meat and making sauces to confit tomatoes and steaming mussels. I prefer a round Dutch oven over an oval to ensure the heat is evenly distributed while it's on the stove or in the oven. Lodge, Le Creuset, and Staub are reliable brands.

Long Tongs

I recommend long sixteen-inch tongs. A set of long tongs gives you the ability to safely maneuver food around a pan without getting splattered by hot oil. OXO makes a great pair with a nonslip handle that I use nearly daily.

Food Processor

This is another investment worth making. I use mine often, for chopping nuts, blending romesco and pesto, and pureeing a chunky soup. If you're debating between a mini and standard size, embrace the cliché: go big or go home. While mini food processors are useful, they're limited in how much they can do.

Digital Thermometer

One of the most commonly asked questions I get from friends is how will they know when meat is done cooking. A digital thermometer takes out the guesswork. While I've listed visual cues in these recipes to indicate when food is perfectly cooked—a crispy edge or golden-brown crust—I've also included the food's desired internal temperature so you can be sure what you're making isn't under- or overdone.

Silicone Spatula

A chef friend of mine once said their spatula was worth its weight in gold. A bit dramatic, but if you have a good one for long enough, it's probably true. A good spatula can help you scoop and scrape every last drop, reducing waste and therefore money. I prefer silicone for its flexibility and durability.

Kitchen Shears

I often reach for my sturdy pair of kitchen shears. It's not worth roughing up your everyday scissors when you want to spatchcock a chicken or trim a bushel of carrot tops.

Fine-Mesh Sieve

A large fine-mesh sieve goes where a colander can't. It allows you to do everything from rinsing canned beans and blanching vegetables to making your own ricotta.

Glass Storage Containers

From pickles and leftovers to sauces and spreads, I've always got a handful of storage containers floating around the refrigerator. Purge your mismatched plastic containers and invest in a good glass set that's long lasting and dishwasher safe. This also helps cut down on the amount of plastic wrap you'll use (at least it has for me).

RETURN OF THE VICTORY GARDEN

In 2020, as the COVID-19 pandemic kept us at home and away from the grocery store, victory gardens—in many cases grown on windowsills—took the country by storm for the first time in decades. The term came about during the First World War when the American government asked citizens to use any available space to grow vegetables, creating more food security during a time of need. If you want to grow vegetables, you should try it. I recommend starting with tomatoes and salad greens such as mesclun and mizuna, which you can find at your local plant shop, along with some hardy herbs like rosemary and thyme. But easier still is *regrowing* vegetables. I know that regrowing a few vegetables probably won't change your shopping habits drastically, but there is something so satisfying about it and worth trying at least once. Below are a few you can try. You'll notice that the principle is basically the same regardless of the vegetable. Make sure to change the water daily to promote healthy growth.

Scallions

Save at least one inch of the white root end of scallions and place them in a cup or jar. Fill the jar with water until the roots are just covered. Scallions can continue to be regrown over and over. Use the scallions for the Black Garlic Butter Salmon with Scallions (page 163) or the Whipped Feta and Charred Scallion Dip (page 35).

Celery

Cut off two inches from the base of the celery (the tough, lighter colored end) and place it in a shallow container. Fill the container with water so half of the celery is submerged. While a celery stalk might take weeks to grow, tender celery leaves will sprout quickly. Use them for the Celery Salad with Walnuts and Pecorino (page 63), or add them to the Everyday Green Salad (page 56).

Carrots

Slice one inch off the top of the carrot, where the leaves are, and place it in a shallow bowl. Fill the bowl halfway with water so half of the carrot is submerged. The carrot won't regrow, but the leafy green tops will. The same method can be used for radishes, turnips, and beets. Use them for the Orecchiette with Carrot Top Pesto and Peas (page 113).

Lettuce

Trim a few inches off the base of the lettuce, where all the leaves connect, and place it in a small bowl. Fill the bowl halfway with water. You'll have some new leaves in a few weeks. Try this with romaine, butter lettuce, or Little Gems and use them in the Green Goddess Salad (page 53), BLT Salad (page 57), or the Everyday Green Salad (page 56).

Lemongrass

Take two inches from a fresh lemongrass stalk and place it in a tall container. Fill halfway with water. A new stalk will grow from the center of the plant. Use lemongrass in the Pork Shoulder Larb (page 151), or make Syrups (page 242).

Tender Herbs

Strip the stem of a tender herb like basil, cilantro, parsley, or mint, leaving the bushy leaves at the top intact. Place it in a glass, making sure that the bushy leaves are sticking out of the top of the glass. Fill the glass with water. The leaves will regrow along the stem, but you'll also see a roots form at the base of the stem, at which point you can repot the tender herb in soil. I use herbs in so many recipes, but a few of my favorites are the Green Goddess Salad (page 53), Greens Skillet Pie (page 83), or the Crispy Rice Salad (page 121).

Potatoes

You know when you've forgotten about a bag of potatoes in a dark bin in the cabinet and then discover that they're covered with sprouts? Those "eyes," or growths, on the potatoes mean that you can replant them. You can try this in a pot, but it's helpful to have some space in a garden, as potatoes tend to spawn multiples underground. Simply make an indent in the soil, place the potato there, and cover with soil. You can do this with a whole potato or cut a piece with an eye if you're looking to plant multiples. It's time to harvest your potatoes when you see the plant start to flower and when some of its leaves begin to turn yellow. Use potatoes for the Fingerling Potato and Leek Top Frittata (page 215) or the Smashed Potato Salad (page 81).

SNACKS AND SPREADS

Aioli

Poached Shrimp with Thousand Island Dressing

This Is How You Make a Cheese Plate

Marinated Red Peppers on Toast

Buttermilk Ricotta with Honey and Toasted Macadamia Nuts

Cheesy Pie Dough Crackers

Marinated Ricotta Salata with Cracked Spices

Whipped Feta and Charred Scallion Dip

Yogurt Chive Flatbread

Crunchy Squash Seeds

Dates Stuffed with Caramelized Onions and Manchego

Fried Sage Leaves

Sweet and Salty Nut Mix

Mixed Olive Tapenade

Curry Butter Popcorn

Crispy Sweet Potato Skins with Crème Fraîche

Aioli

Makes 1 scant cup

Aioli might seem fancy, but it really couldn't be easier to whip together. Served alongside a spread of in-season produce, this garlicky dip is a personal favorite.

A few tips: Add the oil drop-by-drop to ensure the aioli emulsifies and properly thickens. This can take some practice, but I promise if you take it slow you'll soon be able to make aioli in your sleep. And the oil you use makes a difference, too. I like the combination of olive oil and grapeseed oil. Using olive oil alone will result in a flavor that's a little too bitter.

Serve the aioli with a few grinds of black pepper and a spread of raw, roasted, or blanched vegetables (a combination is great for some variety). This is a good time to use up vegetables that you have left over in too-small proportions to do much with, like a handful of snap peas, an endive or two, a few cherry tomatoes, or a lone watermelon radish.

INGREDIENTS

2 egg yolks
1 medium garlic clove, grated
1 teaspoon Dijon mustard
½ teaspoon kosher salt
⅛ teaspoon freshly ground black pepper
¼ cup olive oil
¼ cup grapeseed oil
Juice of 1 lemon

DIRECTIONS

In a medium bowl, combine the egg yolks, garlic, Dijon, salt, and pepper, and whisk to combine.

Add a few drops of olive oil and whisk to combine. Drop by drop, add the olive oil, whisking until the mixture begins to emulsify and thicken. Slowly add the rest of the olive oil, whisking to combine. Drizzle in the grapeseed oil, whisking to combine and thicken.

Add the lemon juice and whisk to combine. Adjust seasonings to taste. Serve the aioli with assorted vegetables. The aioli can be made up to 2 days in advance and stored in a sealed container in the refrigerator.

Need to use up those egg whites? Check out the Orange Meringue Semifreddo (page 189) or Coconut Ginger Pecan Granola (page 209).

Poached Shrimp with Thousand Island Dressing

Serves 4 to 6

Maybe it stems from my mother's love of dunking fries in mayonnaise (she's Dutch, and it's a thing), but when it comes to condiments, mayo rules supreme in my world. It makes just about everything better, from a slice of juicy, ripe tomato to a perfectly poached shrimp. And while I love that classic steak house–style appetizer, once I swapped out cocktail sauce for Thousand Island dressing—with lots of mayo, of course—there was no turning back. Here, the sauce's creaminess is cut by the acidity of the pickles and vinegar, which makes the whole thing balanced . . . and delicious. Besides, it's also a great way to use up half-empty condiment bottles hanging out in the back of the fridge.

Burgers are an obvious choice to use up any extra Thousand Island dressing you might have left over, but I love it smeared on an eight-minute egg, slathered on corn cobs for Mexican-style elote (street corn), and served next to a good steak, too. Shrimp can be poached in water and salt, but aromatics really enhance the flavor without adding much work. Nearly any combination of aromatics will serve—and this is a great place to use up what's in your fridge. Garlic, onions, leeks, bay leaves, celery, parsley, and dill are all great add-ins.

INGREDIENTS

Thousand Island Dressing
¾ cup mayonnaise
¼ cup ketchup
2 tablespoons finely chopped dill pickles
1 garlic clove, minced
2 teaspoons champagne vinegar

Poached Shrimp
2 tablespoons kosher salt
1 teaspoon black peppercorns
Peels of 1 lemon
Juice of 1 lemon
½ cup dry white wine, such as sauvignon blanc or pinot grigio, optional
1½ pounds tail-on shrimp, peeled and deveined

DIRECTIONS

Make the Thousand Island dressing: In a medium bowl, whisk the mayonnaise, ketchup, pickles, garlic, and vinegar to combine. Store in the refrigerator until ready to serve.

Make the poached shrimp: Prepare an ice bath by filling a large bowl with cold water and a few handfuls of ice and set aside. Fill a medium pot with cold water. Add the salt, peppercorns, lemon peels, lemon juice, and wine, if using, to the pot and bring to a boil over medium-high heat. The water should slowly come to a boil so there is time for the aromatics to infuse.

Add the shrimp and remove the pot from the heat. Let the shrimp sit in the water for about 3 minutes, or until pink and opaque. Drain the shrimp through a colander, then transfer to the ice bath for at least 10 minutes. Drain the shrimp from the ice bath.

The shrimp can be made up to 24 hours in advance and kept in the refrigerator in a sealed container. The Thousand Island dressing can be made up to 3 days in advance and kept in the refrigerator in a sealed container. Serve the shrimp with Thousand Island dressing on the side.

Extra Thousand Island dressing? Check out the Smash Burger (page 141). If you buy your shrimp unpeeled, save your shells for the Shrimp Stock (page 236).

THIS IS HOW YOU MAKE A CHEESE PLATE

A cheese plate can be a full spread for a party, like the one in this photo, or an easy meal for one (perfect for days when you really don't feel like cooking). Either way, it's a great way to use up what you already have on hand, like that handful of grapes in your fruit bowl or the last half of a hard salami.

These odds and ends can always feel special—the trick is how you put them together. A few radishes suddenly look very chic and French next to a smear of butter topped with flaky sea salt, and no one will notice that you had only half a jar of pickles left if you serve them in a small bowl. Thinly slice that hard salami or layer prosciutto in ribbons to create visual abundance.

Here's what you need to know before assembling your own cheese board.

First, let's talk cheese. The amount of people you're serving will dictate how much cheese you need, but regardless, you want to consider a mix of texture and type of cheese. In terms of texture, there should be at least one soft, like Brie or burrata; one semifirm, like Gruyère, Stilton, Manchego, or cheddar; and one hard cheese, like Mimolette, Comté, or aged Gouda—but from there, choose what you like. In terms of type, you can think about including cow's, sheep's, and goat's milk cheese for some variety.

Take the cheese out of the refrigerator thirty minutes before serving to let it come to room temperature, where the flavors will be at their peak.

Next, choose an accompaniment or two. I often eat cheese as is (I mean, who can resist nibbling on a hunk of salty Parm?), but for a cheese plate, think about what you'd like to eat it on. I like having a mix of crusty bread and crackers. If you opt for crackers, get a few different sizes and flavors, like ones flecked with herbs or sprinkled with seeds.

Lean into your pantry staples. I'm talking canned fish, pickles (I like French cornichons for their size and bite), olives (I like a mix of green and black), honey, jam (any flavor will work), a pat of room-temperature butter, or whatever else you already have around. These staples enhance your cheese plate in terms of flavor and texture, while simultaneously using the remnants of your pantry.

Marinated Red Peppers on Toast

Serves 4

This is so simple you can barely call it a recipe, but marinated peppers are here for two good reasons. First, roasting bell peppers transforms them completely. A glug of olive oil, splash of vinegar, and thinly sliced shallot make a quick vinaigrette, brightening the sweet and smoky flavor of the peppers into something truly addictive. I add the parsley stems for some added texture and a more concentrated parsley flavor. Second, I don't know about you, but so often I've found one or two peppers lingering at the bottom of the crisper without much inspiration for what to do with them. You can make this whether you have one or five peppers; just scale the recipe as needed. That's why it's a keeper.

Use marinated red peppers in a pasta sauce, serve with hot Italian sausages, use it for a cheese spread, or on sandwiches (my favorite combo layers nutty Manchego and peppery greens with punchy peppers).

INGREDIENTS

4 red bell peppers
1 tablespoon olive oil
½ teaspoon kosher salt
1 small shallot, thinly sliced
2 tablespoons sherry vinegar
½ bunch parsley, leaves and
    tender stems chopped
4 slices sourdough bread,
    lightly toasted

DIRECTIONS

Preheat the oven to 400°F.

Place the peppers on a rimmed baking sheet and drizzle with the olive oil. Use your hands to rub the oil evenly over the peppers. Roast for 25 minutes, then flip with tongs. Continue roasting for about another 15 minutes, or until the peppers are charred all over with wrinkling skin. Take out the peppers and let them cool to room temperature.

Once the peppers are cooled, pull off the stem along with the seeds and discard. Pour off any excess liquid that collects in the peppers and discard that, too. Quarter the peppers and transfer to a bowl. Add the salt, shallot, vinegar, and parsley and toss to combine.

Serve the marinated peppers on top of the toasted sourdough.

There are so many ways to use the rest of the parsley. Check out the Squash with Herby Salsa Verde (page 101), Greens Skillet Pie (page 83), Bucatini with Tuna and Olives (page 107), Roasted Radishes and Turnips with Brown Butter Caper Sauce (page 91), Spicy Brothy Bacony Beans (page 115), Crispy Chicken Thighs with Chickpeas and Olives (page 133), Herby Chicken Salad (page 134), or Red Wine Braised Short Rib Ragout (page 137).

Buttermilk Ricotta with Honey and Toasted Macadamia Nuts

Makes 1 cup

I have yet to find a recipe that uses a whole container of buttermilk. It's not that there's a lack of ways to use it, but most recipes call for a scant amount. This ricotta uses a whopping cup of buttermilk, putting a big dent in that container. (If you don't have buttermilk but still want to make ricotta, just use whole milk.)

The honey and macadamia nuts make this ideal for an appetizer along with some crusty bread, but you could also skip the toppings and mix this into pasta—orecchiette or gemelli would work well (or any other shape where the ricotta can cling to the pasta)—for a main.

INGREDIENTS

3 cups whole milk
1 cup buttermilk
Juice of 1 lemon
1 teaspoon kosher salt
¼ cup macadamia nuts, roughly chopped
1 tablespoon honey
1 tablespoon olive oil
Flaky sea salt, to serve

DIRECTIONS

Line a fine-mesh sieve with cheesecloth and set over a large bowl.

Add the whole milk and buttermilk to a large pot and warm over medium heat until just barely at a simmer. The milk mixture will start to appear thicker. Reduce the heat to medium-low and add the lemon juice and salt, stirring to combine. Reduce the heat to low and simmer for about 5 minutes, or until visibly curdled.

Remove the pot from the heat and let stand at room temperature for about 10 minutes, or until the curdles look even chunkier. Gently pour the mixture into the cheesecloth-lined fine-mesh sieve set over the bowl.

Drain the ricotta for 15 minutes. Discard the whey (the liquid that collects at the bottom of the bowl). Transfer the ricotta to a serving bowl. Alternatively, the ricotta will keep in a sealed container in the refrigerator for up to 3 days.

Meanwhile, heat a small pan over medium heat. Once the pan is hot, add the macadamia nuts and toast for about 2 minutes, stirring often, or until fragrant and golden brown. Transfer the nuts to a plate to cool to room temperature.

Top the ricotta with the toasted nuts, drizzle with the honey and olive oil, and sprinkle with flaky sea salt.

There's always leftover buttermilk. For a savory preparation, try the BLT Salad (page 57). For a sweet one, try the Buttermilk Shortcakes with Roasted Strawberries (page 181). Use those macadamia nuts for a variation on the Coconut Ginger Pecan Granola (page 209), Baklava (page 199), or Sweet and Salty Nut Mix (page 43).

Cheesy Pie Dough Crackers

Serves 8

If you're making a pie and have scraps left over, you're moments away from your very own impossibly addictive, flaky cheesy crackers. I like using cheddar, which makes these taste like a riff on Cheez-Its, but Gruyère, Monterey Jack, or aged Gouda would all work. I've provided a recipe for a full batch of dough here if you want to serve a crowd, but if you're looking to use scraps from the recipes in this book, knead in roughly half the amount of cheddar for the amount of dough you have left. Don't forget to chill it before rolling the dough back out.

INGREDIENTS

1½ cups all-purpose flour, plus more for dusting

1 teaspoon kosher salt

½ teaspoon freshly ground black pepper

½ cup (1 stick) unsalted butter, cold and cubed

1 cup grated cheddar cheese

¼ cup ice water

DIRECTIONS

In the bowl of a food processor, add the flour, salt, and the pepper and pulse three times to combine. Add the butter and pulse until broken down to the size of lima beans. The bigger the pieces of butter, the flakier the dough will be. Add the cheddar and pulse until just combined. Slowly drizzle in the ice water, 1 tablespoon at a time, until the dough just starts to hold together.

Turn out the dough onto a lightly floured surface and shape into a 5-inch disk. Cover with plastic wrap and refrigerate for at least 30 minutes. The dough can be made up to 2 days in advance.

Preheat the oven to 400°F. Line a baking sheet with parchment paper.

On a lightly floured work surface, roll the dough into a 14-inch square. Cut the crackers into 1-inch squares and pierce a hole in the middle of each with a skewer or fork to prevent the crackers from puffing up too much while baking. Transfer the crackers to the prepared baking sheet.

Bake until puffed and golden brown, about 20 minutes. Crackers stay fresh for up to 1 week in a sealed container at room temperature.

Note: If you don't have a food processor, you can make the dough by hand. In a large bowl, whisk the flour, salt, and pepper to combine. Add the butter and use your hands to incorporate the butter into the flour mixture, until the butter pieces are the size of lima beans. Add the cheddar cheese and toss to combine. Add the ice water 1 tablespoon at a time and use your hands to combine, lightly kneading until the dough just starts to hold together.

These crackers can be made using extra dough from the Tomato and Caramelized Onion Galette (page 69), or the Root Vegetable Pot Pie (page 88). Use up that cheddar with the Cauliflower and Cheddar Strata (page 221).

Marinated Ricotta Salata
with Cracked Spices

Serves 4 to 6

Feta has more flavor, and cotjia has more tang, but I love the saltiness of ricotta salata. It's a sheep's milk cheese made from salting fresh ricotta, but unlike the fresh stuff, ricotta salata can be cut into slivers that melt in your mouth. Thinly sliced and drenched in olive oil and aromatics, ricotta salata transforms into a downright addictive snack.

INGREDIENTS

1 teaspoon coriander seeds
1 teaspoon black
    peppercorns
6 ounces ricotta salata, thinly
    sliced
4 sprigs thyme
¼ teaspoon crushed red
    pepper flakes
Peel of 1 lemon, thinly sliced
½ cup olive oil

DIRECTIONS

Place a small pan over medium-high heat. Once the pan is warm, add the coriander seeds and peppercorns and cook until fragrant and toasted, about 1 minute.

Place the toasted coriander seeds and peppercorns in a mortar and use a pestle to grind the seeds until they're roughly cracked. Alternatively, use the back of a chefs' knife to crush the seeds on a cutting board.

Add the ricotta salata to a bowl and sprinkle with cracked coriander and peppercorns, thyme, red pepper flakes, and lemon peel. Drizzle the olive oil over the top and cover with plastic wrap. Let marinate in the refrigerator for at least 1 hour, up to 24 hours, before serving. Marinated ricotta salata lasts for up to a week in the refrigerator.

Serve with bread, crackers, or eat as is.

Use the rest of the thyme from this bunch in the Root Vegetable Pot Pie (page 88), Butter-Basted Lamb Chops (page 155), Chicken Stock (page 234), or White Wine Braised Leeks (page 75).

Whipped Feta and Charred Scallion Dip

Makes 1 cup

I love charred scallions. I blister them in the broiler until they're almost burned; that's when the scallion's peppery flavor mellows into something that's smoky and a little sweet. Once the scallions are blended with feta and lime juice, this turns into my ideal dip. Think of this as the grown-up, cool cousin to the ever-popular onion dip. It's salty, zesty, and of course, cheesy.

INGREDIENTS

2 bunches (about 10) scallions
1 tablespoon olive oil
¾ teaspoon kosher salt, divided
5.5 ounces feta, crumbled (about 1 cup)
½ cup sour cream
½ teaspoon freshly ground black pepper
¾ teaspoon smoked paprika
Zest and juice of 1 lime

DIRECTIONS

Set the oven to broil on high.

Place the scallions on a rimmed baking sheet and drizzle with the olive oil and sprinkle with ½ teaspoon of salt. Use your hands and toss to coat the scallions.

Broil until the scallions are charred all over, about 5 minutes. Let the scallions cool for 5 minutes. Take ¾ of the scallions and chop into ¼-inch slices, discarding the root end. Reserve the remaining ¼ of whole, charred scallions.

In the bowl of a food processor, add the feta and sour cream and blend until smooth. Add the remaining ¼ teaspoon of salt, the pepper, paprika, lime zest and juice, and chopped scallions, and pulse until just combined. Transfer the feta dip to a serving bowl and top with the remaining charred scallions.

The Marbled Sour Cream Coffee Cake (page 200) is an excellent way to use up any leftover sour cream. You can also try the Tomato and Caramelized Onion Galette (page 69); Snap Pea, Daikon, and Fennel Slaw (page 77); or the Fingerling Potato and Leek Top Frittata (page 215).

Yogurt Chive Flatbread

Makes 8 flatbreads

The first time I made flatbread was a revelation—I couldn't believe how easy it was and how good it tasted. The yogurt makes this dough supple, resulting in an almost pillowy texture when fried. But the real joy of this recipe is that it's a blank canvas in terms of flavor. I like chives, but you could add nearly any other herb you have on hand, or one teaspoon of spices like black pepper, turmeric, or crushed red pepper flakes. Sour cream also works in place of yogurt if that's what you have. The joy of flatbreads is that they can be imperfect in shape and still taste delicious, so don't stress too much if they look a little more rustic.

INGREDIENTS

1 cup plus 2 tablespoons all-purpose flour, plus more for dusting

1½ teaspoons baking powder

1 teaspoon kosher salt

1 cup plain whole milk yogurt

¼ cup finely chopped chives

Cooking spray or olive oil, for greasing

DIRECTIONS

In a medium bowl, combine the flour, baking powder, and salt.

Add the yogurt and chives and use your hands to knead the mixture until a ball forms. The dough may feel too sticky at first, but keep kneading to incorporate all of the flour and it'll come together. Cover the bowl with a kitchen towel and let the dough rest for 15 minutes. This will make it easier to roll out.

Line a baking sheet with parchment paper.

Generously flour a clean work surface. Divide the dough into eight equal portions and press each one into a disk using the palm of your hand. Roll each disk into a 6-inch circle and place it on the prepared baking sheet to prevent the flatbread from getting too sticky while you cook them off one by one.

Heat a cast iron or stainless steel pan over medium-high heat and spray with cooking spray. Alternatively, you can add a thin layer of olive oil. Working one at a time, place a disk to the pan and cook for 1 to 2 minutes, until the dough puffs up and is golden in spots. Flip the flatbread with tongs and cook for another minute, until equally spotted. Repeat with the remaining flatbread, adding more cooking spray as needed.

Flatbread is best served immediately.

The rest of the yogurt can be used for the Green Goddess Salad (page 53); Snap Pea, Daikon, and Fennel Slaw (page 77); Chilled Green Soup (page 97); or the Fingerling Potato and Leek Top Frittata (page 215). Or just eat it topped with the Coconut Ginger Pecan Granola (page 209).

Crunchy Squash Seeds

Makes ¼ cup

If you're planning on roasting squash for dinner, don't forget to save the seeds! I'll be honest: cleaning squash seeds is pretty tedious. If you're willing to do the work though, you'll be rewarded with this crunchy snack. While you can eat them as is, I like using them as a topping on something creamy—like yogurt, sour cream, labneh, and crème fraîche—and alongside something crispy, like cucumbers, radishes, and carrots.

From one acorn squash you should get about ¼ cup of seeds, but depending on the type of squash you use, the yield will differ. This preparation can be done with any type of squash, but if you use something like delicata or honeynut, make sure to keep an eye on the smaller seeds—they'll roast faster.

INGREDIENTS
¼ cup acorn squash seeds
2 teaspoons olive oil
½ teaspoon kosher salt
1 teaspoon honey
¼ teaspoon ground sumac

DIRECTIONS
Preheat the oven to 325°F.

Place the squash seeds in a bowl of water and pull off any pulp. Transfer the seeds to a paper towel–lined cutting board and blot dry. The drier you can get the seeds, the crispier they'll become in the oven.

In a medium bowl, add the olive oil, salt, honey, and sumac, and whisk to combine. Add the dried seeds to the bowl and stir until just combined.

Spread the seed mixture onto a rimmed baking sheet in an even layer. Transfer the baking sheet to the oven and roast until golden brown, about 10 minutes. Let the squash seeds cool to room temperature. Store in a sealed container at room temperature for up to 1 week.

If you're using the seeds for this snack, make the Squash with Herby Salsa Verde (page 101).

Dates Stuffed with Caramelized Onions and Manchego

Serves 8

If you're taking the time to make a batch of caramelized onions, make extra for a riff on devils on horseback, swapping out blue cheese for Manchego. They're sweet, salty, and the best part is, they can be made ahead. If you don't have Manchego, try another tangy hard cheese like sharp cheddar, pecorino, or even ricotta salata.

INGREDIENTS

2 tablespoons olive oil
2 tablespoons unsalted butter
4 medium yellow onions, thinly sliced
2 teaspoons sherry vinegar
½ teaspoon kosher salt
2 cups dates, pitted
½ cup Manchego, broken into ½-inch pieces

DIRECTIONS

In a large pan over medium-high heat, add the olive oil and butter. Once the butter melts, add half of the onions and cook for about 2 minutes, stirring occasionally, or until the onions have softened and reduced by half. Add the remaining onions and cook for another 2 minutes, stirring occasionally. Reduce the heat to medium-low and cook for 1 hour, stirring occasionally. Add the vinegar and salt and continue cooking for about 15 minutes, stirring often and scraping up any brown bits on the bottom of the pan, or until the onions are deeply caramelized. Remove the pan from the heat and let the onions cool to room temperature. Caramelized onions can be stored in a sealed container in the refrigerator for up to 5 days.

Stuff the dates with ½ teaspoon of the caramelized onions, then stick a piece of the Manchego in each.

Got a batch of caramelized onions? Check out the Tomato and Caramelized Onion Galette (page 69). Use up extra Manchego for the Chicory, Grapefruit, and Manchego Salad (page 65).

Fried Sage Leaves

I first tasted fried sage leaves when I was visiting my mom's cousin who lived on a lavender farm in Provence. The farm was flanked by rows upon rows of different kinds of lavender (who knew there was more than one variety?). I'd never been anywhere like it. Every night, we'd eat sage chips before dinner. I'm pretty sure I ate nearly the whole plate by myself. Since then, these have become a snack staple in my house. They take minutes to make and you can even prepare them a few hours ahead. It's also the perfect way to use up that oversize pack of sage that's about to turn in the back of your fridge. You can make it with any amount of sage, just make sure the pan is coated with a thin layer of olive oil before getting started, and don't overcrowd the pan. Eat them for a snack, sprinkle them over polenta, or twirl them into a simple brown butter pasta.

INGREDIENTS
Olive oil
Sage leaves
Kosher salt

DIRECTIONS

Heat a thin layer of olive oil in a small to medium pan, making sure the pan is fully coated with oil, over medium-high heat. Once the oil is nearly smoking, add the sage leaves, making sure not to overcrowd the pan, and fry until the edges of the leaves start to turn a darker green and curl up, 15 seconds. Quickly transfer the sage leaves to a paper towel–lined plate and season with salt to taste. Fried sage leaves can be made up to 1 day ahead and stored in a sealed container at room temperature for 2 days.

Got even more sage? Try the Butter-Basted Lamb Chops (page 155).

Sweet and Salty Nut Mix

Makes 3 cups

If you, too, find mixed nuts kind of boring, this recipe is for you. It's the perfect balance of sweet, salty, and spicy thanks to the combination of maple syrup, crushed red pepper flakes, and just the right amount of salt. While this works particularly well with walnuts, cashews, and pecans, this recipe is ideal for using up any nuts you have on hand, like hazelnuts, pistachios, almonds, peanuts, or macadamia nuts. Just make sure they're roughly the same size (sorry, no slivered almonds here!) or you'll run the risk of burning some.

INGREDIENTS

2 tablespoons packed light brown sugar

2 tablespoons olive oil

2 teaspoons pure maple syrup

1½ teaspoons kosher salt

1 teaspoon crushed red pepper flakes

1 teaspoon paprika

¼ teaspoon cayenne pepper

1 cup raw walnuts

1 cup raw pecans

1 cup raw cashews

DIRECTIONS

Preheat the oven to 300°F. Line a rimmed baking sheet with parchment paper.

In a large bowl, add the brown sugar, olive oil, maple syrup, salt, red pepper flakes, paprika, and cayenne, and whisk to combine. Add the walnuts, pecans, and cashews, and stir until fully coated.

Spread the nut mixture onto the prepared baking sheet and transfer to the oven. Bake until the nuts are fragrant and toasted, about 20 minutes.

Let the nuts cool to room temperature, then transfer to a sealed container. The nuts can be stored in a cool place for up to 1 week.

Extra nuts lying around? Make the Baklava (page 199), Celery Salad with Walnuts and Pecorino (page 63), White Wine Braised Leeks (page 75), Hanger Steak with Walnut Romesco (page 143), One-Bowl Fudgy Brownies (page 195), or Coconut Ginger Pecan Granola (page 209).

Mixed Olive Tapenade

Makes 1⅓ cups

Tapenade was a staple appetizer in the eighties, so I think of it as kind of outdated. But then every time I eat it, I remember that it's actually the perfect snack. Tapenade combines olives, anchovies, and capers, resulting in an umami bomb of savory flavor. I've added Castelvetrano olives here for their mild flavor to help cut down on the saltiness. This is also a great way to use up lingering olives in the fridge and some of those pantry staples in the cabinet. Serving it alongside cheese is the most obvious choice, but I also love slathering it on homemade muffuletta sandwiches, or adding a thin layer to the base of a savory galette topped with juicy heirloom tomatoes and goat cheese.

INGREDIENTS

1 cup pitted kalamata olives

1 cup pitted Castelvetrano olives

1 large garlic clove, roughly chopped

1 tablespoon capers, drained and rinsed

2 anchovies

1 teaspoon Dijon mustard

¼ teaspoon crushed red pepper flakes

¼ cup olive oil

DIRECTIONS

In the bowl of a food processor, add the olives, garlic, capers, anchovies, Dijon, red pepper flakes, and olive oil and pulse to combine until the olives are roughly chopped. The tapenade stays fresh for up to 1 week in a sealed container in the refrigerator.

Save the jar of anchovies for the Green Goddess Salad (page 53), Shaved Zucchini with Bagna Cauda (page 61), or the Red Wine Braised Short Rib Ragout (page 137). Castelvetrano olives are used in the Bucatini with Tuna and Olives (page 107) and the Crispy Chicken Thighs with Chickpeas and Olives (page 133).

Crispy Sweet Potato Skins
with Crème Fraîche

Serves 4

Sweet potato skins are often discarded, but they shouldn't be. They're not only packed with a ton of nutrients, but once they're crisped up, they almost taste like chips—here again, yes I love chips! These get a dollop of crème fraîche (but you could totally use sour cream) and are topped with red onion and herbs (there's the blini inspiration), but as always, you can use what you have on hand. As you riff, I recommend something creamy, something crunchy, and something bright, like yogurt, crumbled bacon, scallions, and even Crunchy Squash Seeds (page 39).

INGREDIENTS

4 sweet potatoes
2 tablespoons olive oil, divided
1 teaspoon kosher salt, divided
½ teaspoon freshly ground black pepper
½ teaspoon paprika
Crème fraîche, to serve
¼ red onion, thinly sliced, to serve
1 tablespoon chopped dill, to serve
1 tablespoon chopped chives, to serve
Flaky sea salt, to serve

DIRECTIONS

Preheat the oven to 400°F.

Use a fork to poke holes all over the sweet potatoes. Place the potatoes on a rimmed baking sheet and rub with 1 tablespoon of olive oil and sprinkle the tops with ½ teaspoon of salt. This will help steam release as the potatoes cook.

Bake the potatoes until easily pierced with a knife, about 1 hour. Let the potatoes cool to room temperature, then transfer them to a cutting board and carefully slice them in half lengthwise. Use a large spoon to scoop out the flesh of the potatoes, leaving ¼ inch of flesh on the skins. If you remove all the flesh the potato skins will burn. Cut the skins in half widthwise, and place them back on the baking sheet. Reserve the sweet potato flesh for another use.

Increase the oven temperature to 450°F. Drizzle the potato skins with the remaining 1 tablespoon of olive oil, remaining ½ teaspoon of salt, the pepper, and paprika. Bake until the potatoes have crisped up but not burned, about 10 minutes.

Top with a dollop of crème fraîche, a few slices of onion, the dill, chives, and flaky sea salt.

I make this recipe after I make the Mashed Sweet Potatoes with Honey Butter and Pickled Chilies (page 92). Save the rest of the red onion for the California Citrus Salad (page 55), Crispy Rice Salad (page 121), Pork Shoulder Larb (page 151), Baja-Style Fish Tacos (page 171), or Tuna and White Bean Salad (page 175). Use up the dill with Israeli Couscous with Herbs (page 125) or the Halibut with Tomatoes and Dill (page 161). Save chives for the Yogurt Chive Flatbread (page 37), Green Goddess Salad (page 53), BLT Salad (page 57), or the Smashed Potato Salad (page 81).

SALADS

Panzanella with Tomatoes, Melon, and Pickled Mustard Seeds

Green Goddess Salad

California Citrus Salad

Everyday Green Salad

BLT Salad

Carrot Ribbon Salad

Shaved Zucchini with Bagna Cauda

Celery Salad with Walnuts and Pecorino

Chicory, Grapefruit, and Manchego Salad

Panzanella with Tomatoes, Melon, and Pickled Mustard Seeds

Serves 4 to 6

Bread salad is my favorite kind of salad. It's an excuse to eat golden, crispy pieces of bread with whatever produce is in season. In fall, there's Brussels sprouts and hazelnuts; in winter, chicories and Parm; and spring brings butter lettuce and radishes. This version is for summer, inspired by one of my favorite Italian snack combinations: prosciutto and melon.

To prepare it, there's no need to use a bread knife—use your hands to tear the bread into bite-size chunks. This ensures perfectly imperfect pieces with edges that get crispy and a middle that remains chewy. I opt for frying the bread here (don't worry, this isn't deep-frying!) so each crouton becomes equally crispy and chewy. I know it seems excessive to blanch the mustard seeds so many times, but if you don't they'll be so acrid they'll be inedible. Blanching removes the bitterness, transforming the seeds into plump pearls that taste both sweet and spicy. If you don't have time to make pickled mustard seeds, just swap in whole grain mustard.

INGREDIENTS

Pickled Mustard Seeds
½ cup mustard seeds
½ cup champagne vinegar
½ cup water
1 tablespoon sugar
2 teaspoons kosher salt

Salad
4 tablespoons olive oil, divided
4 cups roughly torn sourdough bread (from 1 small loaf)
½ teaspoon kosher salt
3 cups (about 1½ pints) cocktail or cherry tomatoes, quartered
3 cups cubed melon of choice (1 small)
4 ounces prosciutto, torn
Flaky sea salt, to serve

DIRECTIONS

Make the pickled mustard seeds: Add the mustard seeds to a small pot and cover with cold water. Set the pot over high heat and bring to a boil. Remove from the heat and drain the mustard seeds through a fine-mesh sieve, and repeat the process four more times. Transfer the seeds to a sealable container.

Add the vinegar, water, sugar, and salt to a small pot and bring to a boil, whisking to dissolve the sugar. This is your pickling liquid. Pour the pickling liquid over the mustard seeds and let sit at room temperature until the seeds are tender and plumped, about 1 hour. Pickled mustard seeds can be kept in a sealed container in the refrigerator for up to 3 months.

Make the salad: Heat 3 tablespoons of olive oil in a large skillet over medium heat. Once the oil begins to shimmer, add the bread and cook, stirring occasionally, until golden brown all over, about 8 minutes. Transfer the bread to a serving plate and sprinkle with the salt.

Top with the tomatoes, melon, and prosciutto. Drizzle with the remaining 1 tablespoon of olive oil, top with the ¼ cup of pickled mustard seeds, and sprinkle with flaky sea salt. Panzanella is best served immediately, as the bread will get soggy overnight in the refrigerator.

Pickled mustard seeds can be used in place of whole grain mustard in the Smashed Potato Salad (page 81); Chicory, Grapefruit, and Manchego Salad (page 65); Everyday Green Salad (page 56); or served alongside Sausage and DIY Kraut (page 145). Slice the rest of the sourdough loaf to serve with Marinated Red Peppers on Toast (page 29), cube them for a Cauliflower and Cheddar Strata (page 221), or make Homemade Bread Crumbs (page 239). This Is How You Make a Cheese Plate (page 27) is a great way to use up extra prosciutto.

Green Goddess Salad

Serves 4 to 6

I'm happiest when I eat a big, leafy green salad once a day. When I'm looking to mix things up a bit from my daily vinaigrette, I opt for this green goddess dressing. It's creamy (always a win in my book), punchy, and herbaceous. The trifecta of tarragon, chives, and basil works particularly well together, but this is a great excuse to use up any other tender herbs you have.

If you have one, use a mini food processor here so you'll have less scraping of the bowl.

INGREDIENTS

Green Goddess Dressing
¾ cup plain whole milk yogurt
¼ cup mayonnaise
2 anchovy fillets, roughly chopped
1 garlic clove, roughly chopped
2 tablespoons roughly chopped tarragon leaves
2 tablespoons roughly chopped chives
½ cup roughly chopped basil leaves
Zest of 1 lemon
½ teaspoon kosher salt
½ teaspoon freshly ground black pepper
2 tablespoons olive oil

Salad
1 head butter lettuce, leaves roughly torn
4 cups (about 10 ounces) watercress
4 radishes, thinly sliced
2 avocados, thinly sliced

DIRECTIONS

Make the green goddess dressing: In the bowl of a food processor, add the yogurt, mayonnaise, anchovies, garlic, tarragon, chives, basil, lemon zest, salt, and pepper, and pulse to combine. Once smooth, add the olive oil and pulse until combined. Makes 1 cup. The dressing can be stored in a sealed container in the refrigerator for up to 3 days.

Make the salad: Place the butter lettuce, watercress, radishes, and avocados on a serving plate and drizzle it with the dressing. Serve immediately.

Leftover herbs can be used in the Herby Chicken Salad (page 134). The rest of the yogurt can be used in the Yogurt Chive Flatbread (page 37), or the Chilled Green Soup (page 97). Use the remaining anchovies for the Shaved Zucchini with Bagna Cauda (page 61), or the Red Wine Braised Short Rib Ragout (page 137). Serve any extra radishes with the Aioli (page 23) or the Whipped Feta and Charred Scallion Dip (page 35).

California Citrus Salad

Serves 4 to 6

I moved to Los Angeles in 2013 for a former boyfriend (who hasn't?) and stayed for seven years. One of the things I love about that city—apart from the endless sunshine, of course—are the citrus trees that dot every corner. This citrus salad immediately brings me back to dinner parties with friends where someone was bound to bring a bag overflowing with grapefruit, oranges, or lemons from their yard. I like using a kaleidoscope of citrus here—although this would work with just one type as well—before dusting it with ground sumac, a Middle Eastern spice, for a little tang.

If you don't have sumac, you can sprinkle the citrus with chili powder or even pimenton, Spanish smoked paprika—both add a bit of a kick and color contrast. While you can eat this right away, I'd recommend waiting at least an hour, as the red onions will get pickled from the acidity of the citrus and lose some their sharpness.

INGREDIENTS

5 blood or navel oranges, grapefruit, in any combination
½ red onion, thinly sliced lengthwise
Olive oil
Flaky sea salt
1 cup (½ bunch) cilantro, rough ends trimmed, stems left intact
Ground sumac

DIRECTIONS

On a cutting board, slice the top and bottom of the citrus to create a flat surface on either end. Stand the flat end of the citrus on the cutting board. Using a sharp chef's knife, carefully slice the rind and pith of the citrus in a downward motion, following the shape of the fruit, until you have removed all of the rind and pith. Slice the citrus horizontally into ¼-inch slices.

On a plate, arrange the citrus slices. Top with the onion, olive oil, and flaky sea salt, and let rest at room temperature for 1 hour. If you want to serve this immediately, cut down on the amount of onion, as it won't have enough time to pickle, and will taste too sharp.

Before serving, top with the cilantro and sumac. The salad can be stored in a sealed container in the refrigerator for up to 2 days, just leave out the cilantro and sumac.

Use the other half of the red onion for the Crispy Sweet Potato Skins with Crème Fraîche (page 47) or Pork Shoulder Larb (page 151). Keep the rinds for Candied Citrus Peels (page 191). Save cilantro for the Carrot Ribbon Salad (page 59), Whole Red Snapper with Cilantro and Lime (page 169), or Baja-Style Fish Tacos (page 171).

Everyday Green Salad

Serves 4 to 6

Growing up with two European parents meant eating salad at the end of every meal, never before or during. Even when I would claim to be full, my parents would insist. These days, I still eat a salad *almost* every night, but it often gets bumped up to the main event.

Shallots are salted for this vinaigrette to cut their sharpness and paired with Dijon mustard (sometimes grainy), champagne vinegar (I find it brighter than balsamic; you could use white wine or sherry vinegar, too), and lots of good olive oil (my favorite is Brightland). Make this dressing in the bottom of your salad bowl and don't toss the salad until right before you serve it—this prevents the greens from wilting and saves you a bowl to clean.

INGREDIENTS

Vinaigrette
1 small shallot, minced (about 1 tablespoon)
½ teaspoon kosher salt
1 teaspoon Dijon mustard
¼ teaspoon freshly ground black pepper
1 teaspoon honey
2 tablespoons champagne vinegar
¼ cup good olive oil

Salad
4 to 6 cups greens of choice

DIRECTIONS

Make the vinaigrette: Place the minced shallot in the bottom of a salad bowl and sprinkle with the salt. Let it rest for at least 10 minutes, or up to an hour. The salt mellows the sharpness of the shallot.

Once the shallot is rested, add the Dijon, pepper, honey, and vinegar, and whisk to combine.

While whisking, drizzle in the olive oil until emulsified. Makes ½ cup. The vinaigrette can be kept in a sealed container in the refrigerator for up to 1 week.

Make the salad: Add the salad greens to the bowl. Toss right before serving.

BLT Salad

Serves 2 to 4

My first job at fifteen was as a dishwasher in a diner in the tiny town of Andes, New York. On busy days, the owner-chef would have me help out in the kitchen. After a few hours flipping pancakes on the griddle and frying eggs in butter, I'd be rewarded with a BLT. I'd slather mayonnaise on a New York–style hard roll and top it with a thick slice of tomato, extra crispy bacon, and iceberg lettuce.

Age has taught me eating BLTs every day isn't a sustainable diet, so when I'm looking for that fix, I try to lighten things up with this *slightly* healthier option. Behold the BLT salad! I love Japanese Kewpie mayonnaise for its tangy flavor (it's made with egg yolks and rice vinegar), but any mayonnaise works just fine here. For this recipe, I start bacon in a cold oven so that the fat slowly renders as the oven heats up, resulting in perfectly crispy bacon.

INGREDIENTS

6 strips bacon

5 slices ciabatta, roughly torn (about 2 cups)

3 tablespoons Kewpie mayonnaise

¼ cup buttermilk

1 garlic clove, grated

¼ teaspoon kosher salt

¼ teaspoon freshly ground black pepper

1 tablespoon thinly sliced chives, plus more to serve

Juice of 1 lemon

4 pieces Little Gems lettuce, leaves separated

1 large tomato, roughly chopped

DIRECTIONS

Place the bacon on a rimmed baking sheet. Place in the oven and turn on the heat to 400°F. Cook the bacon for 18 minutes, or to desired crispiness.

Leave the bacon fat on the baking sheet and transfer the bacon to a paper towel–lined plate to cool to room temperature.

Toss the ciabatta in the bacon fat, and return the baking sheet to the oven for about 10 minutes, or until the ciabatta is golden and crisped.

In a bowl, whisk the mayonnaise, buttermilk, garlic, salt, pepper, chives, and lemon juice to combine.

Toss the Little Gems with the crispy bread, bacon, and tomato. Drizzle the salad with the buttermilk dressing and serve immediately.

Use up buttermilk with the Buttermilk Shortcakes with Roasted Strawberries (page 181), or the Buttermilk Ricotta with Honey and Toasted Macadamia Nuts (page 30). Kewpie mayonnaise is great with the Herby Chicken Salad (page134), where you'll find a recipe for your own version. Save chives for the Yogurt Chive Flatbread (page 37), Green Goddess Salad (page 53), Smashed Potato Salad (page 81), or the Crispy Sweet Potato Skins with Crème Fraîche (page 47). Since you'll have leftover bacon, try making Spicy Brothy Bacony Beans (page 115) or Really Good Meatballs (page 135). You can make Homemade Bread Crumbs (page 239) with leftover ciabatta.

Carrot Ribbon Salad

Serves 4

This surprisingly simple salad combines carrot ribbons with golden raisins, mint, cilantro, and crunchy pita chips before being drizzled with a garlicky dressing. What makes this salad stand out is that every bite is packed with tons of flavor and texture. I love the addition of pomegranate molasses, a staple in Middle Eastern cooking, in the dressing for the earthy sweetness it adds, but if you don't have it, just leave it out.

All the components of this salad can be made in advance, which makes it ideal for dinner parties. Dress the salad right before serving or it'll become too soggy.

INGREDIENTS

3 pitas, torn into 1-inch pieces
¼ cup plus 2 tablespoons olive oil, divided
1½ teaspoons kosher salt, divided
2 bunches medium carrots (about 10)
2 garlic cloves, grated
Zest of 1 lemon
Juice of ½ lemon
1 teaspoon pomegranate molasses
½ teaspoon freshly ground black pepper
1 teaspoon ground sumac
¾ cup golden raisins
¼ cup mint leaves, torn
¼ cup cilantro leaves, torn

DIRECTIONS

Preheat the oven to 350°F.

Place the pita on a rimmed baking sheet and drizzle with the 2 tablespoons of olive oil and season with the ½ teaspoon of salt, and toss with your hands to coat. Bake until the pita is golden brown and crispy, about 10 minutes. Let cool to room temperature.

On a cutting board, use a vegetable peeler to peel the carrots into ribbons. Transfer the carrot ribbons to a large bowl.

In a glass measuring cup or small bowl, add the garlic, lemon zest, lemon juice, pomegranate molasses, the remaining 1 teaspoon of salt, the pepper, and sumac, and whisk to combine. While whisking, drizzle in the ¼ cup of olive oil until emulsified. The dressing can be stored in a sealed container at room temperature for up to 2 weeks.

Add half the toasted pita chips, the raisins, mint, and cilantro to the bowl with the carrot ribbons. Drizzle with the vinaigrette tossing until everything is well coated. Top with the remaining pita chips.

Sometimes I swap out ginger for golden raisins if I have them in the Coconut Ginger Pecan Granola (page 209). Use up mint with the Squash with Herby Salsa Verde (page 101), Crispy Rice Salad (page 121), or Israeli Couscous with Herbs (page 125).

Shaved Zucchini with Bagna Cauda

Serves 4

I think bagna cauda makes nearly everything it touches better. In Italy, where it's traditional, this sauce of garlic and anchovies is often served as an appetizer with raw vegetables, like a crudités plate. Here it dresses paper-thin slices of zucchini and summer squash.

INGREDIENTS

Bagna Cauda
10 garlic cloves
10 anchovy fillets (1 can)
¼ teaspoon kosher salt
¾ cup olive oil
4 tablespoons cold unsalted
  butter

Salad
1 small zucchini, cut into
  ⅟₁₆-inch slices with a
  mandoline or knife
1 small summer squash, cut
  into ⅟₁₆-inch slices with a
  mandoline or knife
1 cup basil leaves
1 ounce Parmesan, sliced into
  slivers (about ¼ cup)
Flaky sea salt
Freshly ground black pepper

DIRECTIONS

Make the bagna cauda: Place the garlic and anchovies on a cutting board and mince together. Sprinkle the mixture with the salt. Then use the back of a chefs' knife to repeatedly press down on the mixture until a paste forms. Transfer the paste into a small pot along with the olive oil, set over medium heat, and bring to a simmer. Reduce the heat to low and simmer for about 10 minutes, stirring occasionally, or until the garlic is fragrant but not yet brown. Add the butter and stir until melted. The bagna cauda can be refrigerated in a sealed container for up to 3 days.

Make the salad: Place the zucchini and squash on a serving platter and scatter the basil over the top. Spoon the bagna cauda over and top with the Parmesan slivers, flaky sea salt, and pepper, and serve immediately.

Parmesan makes just about everything better, too, but I use leftovers often in the Kale with Lemon and Parmesan (page 95), Eggplant Parmesan (page 85), or Really Good Meatballs (page 135). Save the rind for Spicy Brothy Bacony Beans (page 115), Corn Stock (page 235), Chicken Stock (page 234), or Parmesan Broth (page 237). Save basil for Charred Corn and Burrata (page 79), Chilled Green Soup (page 97), Squash with Herby Salsa Verde (page 101), Crispy Rice Salad (page 121), or Herby Chicken Salad (page 134).

Celery Salad with Walnuts and Pecorino

Serves 2 to 4

I always have a bunch of celery in my fridge. I'm grateful to celery for adding a vegetal flavor to Italian sofrito and crunch to tuna salad, but though it excels in these supporting roles, at my house, it's so rarely the star of the show. I wanted to make a dish where celery could shine. Crunchy, creamy, and punchy, this salad hits all the right notes.

INGREDIENTS

¼ cup raw walnuts

1 egg yolk

4 garlic cloves, grated

1 tablespoon Dijon mustard

½ teaspoon salt

¼ teaspoon freshly ground
  black pepper

¼ cup good olive oil

3 tablespoons sherry vinegar

1 bunch celery stalks, sliced
  into ⅛-inch slices on the
  bias, leaves reserved

2 ounces pecorino, thinly
  sliced

DIRECTIONS

Heat a small pan over medium-high heat. Add the walnuts and toast, stirring occasionally, until fragrant, about 2 minutes. Transfer the walnuts to a plate to cool to room temperature. Once cooled, roughly chop and reserve for later.

In a glass measuring cup or small bowl, whisk the egg yolk, garlic, Dijon, salt, and pepper, until smooth. While whisking, drizzle in the olive oil until emulsified. Add the vinegar and whisk to combine. Taste to adjust seasonings. The dressing can be stored in a sealed container in the refrigerator for up to 24 hours.

On a plate, scatter the celery slices and leaves. Pour over the dressing, top with the pecorino and walnuts and serve immediately.

Celery adds a great crunch in the Tuna and White Bean Salad (page 175). You can also use it for the Corn Soup with Garlic Chips (page 99), or Chicken Stock (page 234). Save the leftover egg white for Coconut Ginger Pecan Granola (page 209) or the Orange Meringue Semifreddo (page 189). Walnuts can be saved for the Hanger Steak with Walnut Romesco (page 143), White Wine Braised Leeks (page 75), or the One-Bowl Fudgy Brownies (page 195). You can also save the Pecorino rind and add it to the Parmesan Broth (page 237)—while the flavor is tangier, in the broth you won't notice the difference.

Chicory, Grapefruit, and Manchego Salad

Serves 4 to 6

Winter doesn't have to mean a season without greens. Chicories, which thrive in cooler months, are a family of vibrantly colored lettuces, including radicchio, frisée, endive, escarole, and puntarelle. I like using a mix of a few kinds for this salad for different texture and color variation, but you can also use whatever chicory you have on hand. Depending on the variety, some are more bitter than others. But the dressing here is almost sweet and, when paired with toasted hazelnuts and slices of Manchego, helps cut the bitterness of the chicory.

This recipe uses black garlic, which is garlic that's been aged and fermented until the cloves soften and turn black. The flavor is sweet, almost syrupy—it's garlic without any of the sharpness. You can find black garlic at specialty grocers or online. Alternatively, this recipe can be made by swapping the black garlic with one minced garlic clove and one teaspoon of maple syrup.

INGREDIENTS

¼ cup hazelnuts

1 grapefruit

2 large black garlic cloves

1 teaspoon whole grain mustard

3 tablespoons olive oil

6 cups (2 to 3 heads) mixed chicory, roughly torn

2 ounces Manchego, thinly sliced (about ½ cup)

Flaky sea salt, to serve

DIRECTIONS

Heat a small pan over medium-high heat. Once the pan is warm, add the hazelnuts and cook until fragrant, about 2 minutes. Transfer the hazelnuts to a kitchen towel and rub the towel together until most of the papery skins fall off. Roughly chop the hazelnuts on a cutting board.

On a cutting board, slice the top and bottom of the grapefruit to create a flat surface on either end. Place the citrus on one flat surface onto the cutting board. Using a sharp chef's knife, carefully slice the rind and pith of the citrus in a downward motion, following the shape of the fruit, until you have removed all of the rind and pith. Carefully slice each grapefruit segment to release it from the membrane. Squeeze the membrane and any remaining grapefruit into the bowl, which should give you about 2 tablespoons of grapefruit juice.

Finely chop the garlic on a cutting board. Then use the back of your knife to press down on the garlic until it forms a paste. Transfer the garlic to a large bowl along with the 2 tablespoons of grapefruit juice and the mustard, and whisk until smooth. While whisking, slowly drizzle in the olive oil until emulsified. The vinaigrette can be stored in a sealed container at room temperature for up to 2 weeks.

Add the chicory and grapefruit segments to the bowl and toss with the vinaigrette until well combined. Top with the hazelnuts, the Manchego, and flaky sea salt, and serve immediately.

Use up extra black garlic with the Black Garlic Butter Salmon with Scallions (page 163). Manchego can be used in the Dates Stuffed with Caramelized Onions and Manchego (page 40). Swap in hazelnuts for pecans in the Coconut Ginger Pecan Granola (page 209), Baklava (page 189), or Sweet and Salty Nut Mix (page 43).

VEGETABLES

Tomato and Caramelized Onion Galette

Blistered Asparagus and Peas with Salt-Cured Egg Yolks

White Wine Braised Leeks

Snap Pea, Daikon, and Fennel Slaw

Charred Corn and Burrata

Smashed Potato Salad

Greens Skillet Pie

Eggplant Parmesan

Root Vegetable Pot Pie

Roasted Radishes and Turnips with Brown Butter Caper Sauce

Mashed Sweet Potatoes with Honey Butter and Pickled Chilies

Charred Cauliflower with Zhoug and Pine Nuts

Kale with Lemon and Parmesan

Chilled Green Soup

Corn Soup with Garlic Chips

Squash with Herby Salsa Verde

Tomato and Caramelized Onion Galette

Serves 2 to 4

There are few better ways to show off your in-season tomatoes than this stunner. In theory, you could make it for dinner, take leftovers to lunch the next day, eat a slice for breakfast. But I've never had this last for more than twenty-four hours.

The key to making a standout tomato galette is to salt the tomatoes before baking. The salt draws out any excess moisture that could otherwise leave your dough soggy. Also, I call these onions "lightly caramelized" because ideally they'll be more golden than deep brown. Caramelized onions tend to be too sweet to pair with in-season tomatoes, while the lighter version still has some bite.

INGREDIENTS

Tomato Galette

1½ cups all-purpose flour, plus more for dusting

1 teaspoon kosher salt, divided

½ teaspoon freshly ground black pepper

½ cup (1 stick) unsalted butter, cold and cubed

½ cup sour cream, divided

¼ cup ice water

3 medium heirloom or beefsteak tomatoes, cut into ½-inch slices

1 egg

1 tablespoon water

2 teaspoons flaky sea salt

Lightly Caramelized Onions

2 tablespoons olive oil

2 tablespoons unsalted butter

4 medium yellow onions, thinly sliced

2 teaspoons sherry vinegar

½ teaspoon kosher salt

DIRECTIONS

Make the galette: In the bowl of a food processor, add the flour, ½ teaspoon of kosher salt, and the pepper, and pulse three times to combine. Add the butter and pulse to make pieces the size of lima beans. Don't overmix: the bigger the pieces of butter, the flakier the dough will be. Mix ¼ cup of sour cream and the ice water in a glass measuring cup and pour into the flour mixture 1 tablespoon at a time, pulsing between additions, until the dough just starts to hold together.

Turn out the dough onto a lightly floured surface and shape into a 5-inch disk. Cover with plastic wrap and refrigerate for at least 1 hour. The dough can be made up to 2 days in advance and stored in the refrigerator.

Make the caramelized onions: In a large pan over medium-high heat, melt the olive oil and butter. Add half of the onions and cook for about 2 minutes, stirring occasionally, or until the onions have released some of their water and start to soften. Add the remaining onions and cook for 2 minutes, stirring occasionally. Reduce the heat to medium-low and cook until the onions are golden brown and reduced in volume by half, stirring occasionally, about 1 hour. Add the vinegar and salt and continue cooking for about 20 minutes, stirring often and scraping up any brown bits on the bottom of the pan, or until the onions are lightly caramelized. Remove the pan from the heat and let the onions cool to room temperature. The caramelized onions can be stored in a sealed container in the refrigerator for up to 1 week.

While the dough is resting, arrange the tomato slices in a single layer on a paper towel–lined plate and sprinkle with the remaining ½ teaspoon of kosher salt. Let sit for at least 1 hour to draw out excess moisture. Use a paper towel to dab the moisture off the tomatoes.

Continued on next page

Preheat the oven to 400°F.

Lightly flour a sheet of parchment paper. Place the chilled dough on the parchment paper and roll into a 14-inch circle. Transfer the parchment with the dough to a rimmed baking sheet. If the dough is getting warm, return the baking sheet to the refrigerator for at least 10 minutes.

Spread the remaining ¼ cup of sour cream in a circle on the dough, leaving a 2-inch border all around. Spread the caramelized onions on top of the sour cream, then layer the tomatoes on top, overlapping slightly. Fold the edge of the crust over the tomatoes, working your way around and overlapping the crust as needed.

In a small bowl, beat the egg and water to make an egg wash. Brush the crust with the egg wash and sprinkle with the flaky sea salt.

Bake until the crust is golden brown, about 1 hour. Let the galette cool for at least 20 minutes before serving. The galette can be covered and stored at room temperature for up to 3 days.

Note: If you don't have a food processor, you can make the crust by hand. In a large bowl, whisk the flour, salt, and pepper to combine. Add the butter and use your hands to press the butter into the flour, until the pieces of butter are the size of lima beans. Add the sour cream mixture 1 tablespoon at a time and use your hands to combine, lightly kneading until the dough sticks together.

If you decide to make a big batch of caramelized onions, double the recipe and save half for the Dates Stuffed with Caramelized Onions and Manchego (page 40). If you've got excess dough from trimming your galette, make a handful of Cheesy Pie Dough Crackers (page 31). The rest of your sour cream can be used in the Snap Pea, Daikon, and Fennel Slaw (page 77); Marbled Sour Cream Coffee Cake (page 200); Fingerling Potato and Leek Top Frittata (page 215); or the Crunchy Squash Seeds (page 39).

Blistered Asparagus and Peas with Salt-Cured Egg Yolks

Serves 4

This recipe is a true celebration of spring, combining quickly blistered asparagus and peas. The dish gets covered in a layer of shaved salt-cured egg yolk, a Chinese tradition that dates back centuries. Think of it like asparagus with hollandaise 2.0. It's also one of my favorite ways to use up leftover egg yolks. Sure, it takes a bit of planning, but the final result comes together in minutes.

Here's how it works: Egg yolks are submerged in a salt-and-sugar mixture and spend a week—or up to a month—in the fridge. Once they're ready, you just wash off that mixture and they're ready to use. The result is a firm yolk that can be grated like cheese. Add a dusting of salt-cured egg yolks over pasta, vegetables, really whatever you like. Salt kills bacteria during the curing process, but I recommend using pasteurized eggs if you have any health concerns. If you want to make this without the salt-cured egg yolks, grate a generous dusting of Parmesan on top.

INGREDIENTS

Salt-Cured Egg Yolks
3 cups kosher salt
1 cup sugar
6 egg yolks

Asparagus
Juice of 1 lemon
2 teaspoons whole grain mustard
2 tablespoons olive oil
1 bunch asparagus, ends removed
1 cup fresh or frozen (thawed) peas
½ teaspoon kosher salt

DIRECTIONS

Make the salt-cured egg yolks: Add the salt and sugar to the bowl of a food processor and pulse until finely ground. Spread half of the salt mixture onto a 9x9-inch baking dish and make six depressions with the back of a spoon. Gently place the egg yolks into the depressions, and use the remaining salt mixture to cover them. Wrap the baking dish in plastic wrap and transfer to the refrigerator. Refrigerate for 5 to 7 days, until the egg yolks are very firm to the touch. Rinse the yolks with water to remove any excess mixture, and dry with a paper towel. The egg yolks can be stored in a sealed container in the refrigerator for up to 1 month.

Make the asparagus: Grate one salt-cured egg yolk into a small bowl or glass measuring cup using a rasp grater or a box grater. Add the lemon juice and mustard and whisk to combine.

Add the olive oil to a large pan and heat over high heat. Once the oil is shimmering and beginning to smoke, add the asparagus and cook until the asparagus is bright green and charred in spots, shaking the pan occasionally, about 5 minutes. Remove the asparagus and transfer to a serving bowl.

Add the peas to the same pan and cook, without moving, until blistered on one side, about 30 seconds. Spoon the peas on top of the asparagus, and sprinkle with salt, tossing to combine.

Pour the lemon mixture over the asparagus and peas. Grate one more salt-cured egg yolk over the asparagus and serve immediately.

Save egg whites for the Coconut Ginger Pecan Granola (page 209) or the Orange Meringue Semifreddo (page 189).

White Wine Braised Leeks

Serves 2 to 4

Sure, leeks take a few minutes to clean, but it's worth it. Braised in butter and white wine and steeped in garlic and thyme, these leeks become so tender they almost melt in your mouth. Serve them as a side dish all on their own, or chop them up and add to one pound of cooked pasta for a easy weeknight meal.

INGREDIENTS

4 to 5 medium leeks
¼ cup raw walnuts
4 tablespoons unsalted butter, divided
½ teaspoon kosher salt
¼ teaspoon freshly ground black pepper
¼ cup dry white wine, such as sauvignon blanc or pinot grigio
1½ cups vegetable or chicken stock
3 garlic cloves
4 sprigs thyme
1 tablespoon sherry vinegar
Flaky sea salt

DIRECTIONS

On a cutting board, trim the root end and dark leek tops. Slice the leeks in half lengthwise and remove any tough outer leaves. Run the leeks under cold water to wash out any soil, careful to keep the leeks intact. Line a cutting board with paper towels. Transfer the leeks to the paper towel–lined cutting board to dry completely.

Heat a large stainless steel or cast iron pan over medium-high heat. Add the walnuts and toast for about 2 minutes, stirring occasionally, or until the walnuts smell fragrant. Transfer the walnuts to a plate to cool to room temperature. Once cooled, roughly chop and reserve for later.

Add 3 tablespoons of butter to the same pan over medium-high heat. Once the butter melts, add the leeks, cut-side down, and cook for about 3 minutes, or until golden brown.

Carefully flip the leeks with tongs and season with the salt and pepper. Cook the leeks for about another 3 minutes, or until the other side is golden brown.

Add the wine to the pan and cook for about 1 minute, without stirring, or until you can no longer smell the alcohol.

Add the stock, garlic, and thyme to the pan and bring it to a simmer. Place a lid on the pan and reduce heat to medium-low. Cook for about 20 minutes, or until a knife can easily pierce the leeks without any resistance.

Carefully remove the leeks, leaving the liquid in the pan, and set them on a serving plate. Discard the thyme.

Return the pan to medium-high heat. Add the remaining 1 tablespoon of butter and the vinegar and cook the liquid for about 3 minutes, or until reduced by half.

Pour the sauce over the leeks and sprinkle with flaky sea salt and the reserved toasted walnuts. The leeks can be stored in a sealed container in the refrigerator for up to 3 days.

Save the green leek tops for the Fingerling Potato and Leek Top Frittata (page 215). Use the rest of the thyme from this bunch in the Root Vegetable Pot Pie (page 88), Marinated Ricotta Salata with Cracked Spices (page 33), Butter-Basted Lamb Chops (page 155), or Chicken Stock (page 234).

Snap Pea, Daikon, and Fennel Slaw

Serves 4 to 6

Since this dish is all about crunch, the fresher the vegetables you use the better. What I love about this recipe is that you use the fennel bulb, a few fennel stalks (which are often discarded), and even the fennel fronds, the bright green, frilly bits coming off the top of the fennel stalks, which add a subtle anise flavor. If you can't find daikon, a handful of radishes can be swapped in.

INGREDIENTS

8 ounces snap peas, trimmed, thinly sliced on the bias

3 tablespoons sour cream

2 tablespoons olive oil

Zest of 1 lemon

2 tablespoons lemon juice

½ teaspoon kosher salt

3 teaspoons poppy seeds, divided

1 small fennel bulb, thinly sliced (1 cup), 2 stalks thinly sliced

1 small daikon, thinly sliced (about 1 cup)

1 tablespoon fennel fronds, roughly torn

DIRECTIONS

Prepare an ice bath by filling a bowl with cold water and add a handful of ice cubes.

Bring a small pot of salted water to a boil over high heat. Add the snap peas and blanch until bright green and just tender, about 2 minutes. Drain the snap peas in a colander, then transfer to the ice bath for 5 minutes to stop them from cooking. Remove the snap peas from the ice bath and shake off the excess water.

In a medium bowl, add the sour cream, olive oil, lemon zest and juice, salt, and 2 teaspoons of poppy seeds, and whisk to combine.

Add the snap peas, sliced fennel bulb and stalks, and the daikon to the bowl and stir to combine. Top with the remaining 1 teaspoon of poppy seeds and the fennel fronds. The slaw is best served immediately, as the snap peas will start to discolor over time.

This slaw only uses a small bulb of fennel, so if you have a big one, use any leftovers for the Clams with Chorizo and Fennel (page 165). Save leftover fennel stalks to add to the Spicy Brothy Bacony Beans (page 115). Use up sour cream in the Tomato and Caramelized Onion Galette (page 69), Marbled Sour Cream Coffee Cake (page 200), Fingerling Potato and Leek Top Frittata (page 215), or the Crunchy Squash Seeds (page 39). I like topping the Farro Porridge (page 213) with poppy seeds, too.

Charred Corn and Burrata

Serves 4

You can't get more summery than sweet corn. I'm not the first one to put together this combination, but in August, sweet corn paired with a ball of burrata and a handful of basil is all I want to eat. Serve with some bread and call it a day.

INGREDIENTS

2½ tablespoons olive oil, divided

2 medium leeks, white and light green parts thinly sliced

2 medium garlic cloves, minced

6 ears of corn, kernels removed

1 teaspoon kosher salt

½ teaspoon freshly ground black pepper

½ teaspoon crushed red pepper flakes

½ cup basil leaves

8-ounce ball burrata

Flaky sea salt, to serve

DIRECTIONS

Heat 1½ tablespoons of olive oil in a large pan over medium heat. Once the oil begins to shimmer, add the leeks and cook until the leeks soften, but without any color, about 5 minutes. Add the garlic and stir until fragrant, about 1 minute.

Increase the heat to medium-high and add the corn, salt, black pepper, and red pepper flakes, and continue cooking, stirring occasionally, until the corn is lightly charred, 8 to 10 minutes. The charred corn can be stored in a sealed container in the refrigerator for up to 3 days.

Transfer the corn to a serving bowl and top with the basil, burrata, remaining 1 tablespoon of olive oil, and the flaky sea salt. Serve immediately.

Corn cobs can be saved in a freezer bag until you're ready to make the Corn Stock (page 235). Use the Corn Stock to make Corn Soup with Garlic Chips (page 99). Don't toss those green leek tops—use them for the Fingerling Potato and Leek Top Frittata (page 215). If you bought a whole bunch of leeks, and you have one or two left over, use the rest for the White Wine Braised Leeks (page 75) and cut the recipe in half. Save basil for the Chilled Green Soup (page 97), Squash with Herby Salsa Verde (page 101), Crispy Rice Salad (page 121), and Herby Chicken Salad (page 134).

Smashed Potato Salad

Serves 4

I love a smashed potato because it delivers both textures that a potato can: a creamy inside and crispy exterior. There are two rules to follow for a really great smashed potato. First, boil those potatoes until just fork-tender. Then make sure they're as dry as possible before roasting. To do this I usually boil my potatoes a few hours ahead of when I need to use them—sometimes even a day in advance—and keep them in the refrigerator until I'm ready to go.

INGREDIENTS

3 pounds fingerling or new potatoes

2 tablespoons plus 2 teaspoons kosher salt, divided

¾ cup plus 2 tablespoons olive oil, divided

1½ teaspoons freshly ground black pepper

2 tablespoons whole grain mustard

2 tablespoons sherry vinegar

2 garlic cloves, grated

2 tablespoons finely chopped chives

DIRECTIONS

Preheat the oven to 425°F.

Add the potatoes to a large pot and cover with cold water. Add the 2 tablespoons of salt to the pot and bring to a boil over high heat. Boil until the potatoes are just fork-tender, 10 to 12 minutes.

Drain the potatoes through a colander and let them dry completely.

Place the dried potatoes on a rimmed baking sheet. Use a can or flat-bottomed surface (like a measuring cup or jar) to smash the potatoes. The potatoes should smash easily, without much resistance.

Drizzle ½ cup of olive oil over the potatoes, using your hands to toss to combine, and sprinkle with the 1 teaspoon salt and 1 teaspoon pepper.

Roast until the potatoes are crispy on the edges, about 40 minutes.

Meanwhile, add the mustard, vinegar, garlic, chives, the remaining 1 teaspoon of salt and ½ teaspoon of pepper to a medium bowl and whisk to combine. Slowly drizzle in the remaining ¼ cup plus 2 tablespoons of olive oil and whisk until emulsified. Add the potatoes to the bowl and toss until well coated. The potato salad can be stored in a sealed container in the refrigerator for up to 3 days.

If you bought too many potatoes, make the Fingerling Potato and Leek Top Frittata (page 215). Save chives for the Yogurt Chive Flatbread (page 37), Crispy Sweet Potato Skins with Crème Fraîche (page 47), or Green Goddess Salad (page 53).

Greens Skillet Pie

Serves 4

Sometimes I panic that I haven't been eating enough greens and feel the need to rectify it immediately. This skillet pie is basically an excuse to eat a huge amount of greens (go, you!), while still getting to indulge. I like cutting and layering the puff pastry in squares to add some texture, and it looks cool, but you could also just add the sheet in one layer.

If you have other types of greens like spinach, collards, or even radish greens, you can add them here. I like using two colors of sesame seeds, again because it looks cool (and why shouldn't greens look cool?). Feel free to use one kind if that's what you have.

INGREDIENTS

2 tablespoons olive oil

2 large shallots, thinly sliced

1 large bunch Swiss chard, leaves and stems separated and thinly sliced, divided

3 garlic cloves, minced

2 medium bunches Lacinato or dinosaur kale, tough stems removed, leaves thinly sliced

3 cups arugula, roughly chopped

1 cup roughly chopped parsley leaves and stems

½ cup roughly chopped dill

1¼ teaspoons kosher salt

½ teaspoon freshly ground black pepper

All-purpose flour, for dusting

1 sheet puff pastry, thawed

1 large egg beaten with 1 tablespoon water

2 teaspoons sesame seeds

2 teaspoons black sesame seeds

DIRECTIONS

Preheat the oven to 375°F.

Heat the olive oil in a large stainless steel or cast iron pan over medium-high heat. Once the oil begins to shimmer, add the shallots and Swiss chard stems and cook, stirring occasionally, until softened and golden brown at the edges, 4 to 5 minutes.

Add the garlic and cook, stirring occasionally, until fragrant, about 1 minute.

Add the Swiss chard leaves and kale and cook, stirring occasionally, until wilted by half, about 3 minutes.

Remove the pan from the heat and add the arugula, parsley, dill, salt, and pepper, and stir to combine until just wilted.

Lightly flour a clean surface. Place the thawed puff pastry on top of the floured area and use a rolling pin to roll it out to a 12×16-inch rectangle. Cut the pastry into twelve 4-inch squares. Brush the pastry squares with the egg wash.

Layer the puff pastry pieces over the greens, still in the pan, overlapping slightly to make sure the greens are covered. Sprinkle with the sesame seeds.

Bake until the puff pastry is deeply golden brown and puffed, about 45 minutes.

Let the pan cool for 10 minutes. Serve straight from the pan, making sure every scoop has a bit of puff pastry and greens. Greens skillet pie can be covered and stored in the refrigerator for up to 3 days, but be forewarned that the puff pastry will get soggy over time.

Use up dill with Israeli Couscous with Herbs (page 125), Halibut with Tomatoes and Dill (page 161), or Crispy Sweet Potato Skins with Crème Fraîche (page 47). For parsley, check out the Squash with Herby Salsa Verde (page 101), Bucatini with Tuna and Olives (page 107), Roasted Radishes and Turnips with Brown Butter Caper Sauce (page 91), Spicy Brothy Bacony Beans (page 115), Crispy Chicken Thighs with Chickpeas and Olives (page 133), Herby Chicken Salad (page 134), or Red Wine Braised Short Rib Ragout (page 137).

Eggplant Parmesan

Serves 6 to 8

I've found the best way to please a group of people with various diets and preferences is to pull a piping hot tray of eggplant Parmesan out of the oven. It's vegetarian, feeds a crowd, and there's nothing more comforting when the weather turns cooler.

The two wins here are that although this recipe is time consuming, you can make it over multiple days and even assemble the whole thing ahead. Frying the eggplant in panko yields an extra crispy eggplant with no sogginess. (I recommend taking a break mid–eggplant frying to eat one sans sauce.)

INGREDIENTS

Sauce
2 tablespoons olive oil
4 tablespoons unsalted butter
2 yellow onions, finely chopped
4 garlic cloves, minced
1 can (6 ounces) tomato paste
1 teaspoon crushed red pepper flakes
3 teaspoons kosher salt, plus more to taste
1 teaspoon freshly ground black pepper
2 cans (28 ounces each) whole tomatoes
One 14.5-ounce can whole tomatoes

Eggplant
2 large globe eggplants, cut into ¼-inch slices lengthwise
1½ teaspoons kosher salt, plus more for salting the eggplant
1 cup all-purpose flour
1 teaspoon freshly ground black pepper
4 eggs
4 cups panko
¾ cup olive oil
1½ cups grated Parmesan
2 balls (8 ounces each) fresh mozzarella, cut into ¼-inch slices

DIRECTIONS

Make the sauce: In a large Dutch oven, heat the olive oil and butter over medium heat. Once the butter is melted, add the onions and cook for about 30 minutes, stirring occasionally, or until the onions have released some of their water, have softened, and become golden. Add the garlic and stir for about 3 minutes, or until fragrant. Increase the heat to medium-high, add the tomato paste, and stir until the paste turns brick red and caramelizes, about 3 minutes.

Add the red pepper flakes, salt, and the black pepper, and stir to combine. Squeeze the tomatoes with your hands into the pot to crush them. Pour in the remaining tomato juice from the can. Bring to a boil, then reduce the heat and simmer for 30 minutes. Let cool to room temperature. Salt to taste.

Make the eggplant: Meanwhile, line a cutting board or rimmed baking sheet with paper towels. Arrange the eggplant slices in a single layer on the paper towel–lined surface and sprinkle with salt. Let sit for 1 hour, until you see droplets of water on top of the eggplant. Use a paper towel to blot the eggplant.

Place the flour, the 1½ teaspoons of salt, and pepper in a shallow bowl and whisk to combine. In a second shallow bowl, add the eggs and beat. In a third shallow bowl, add the panko. Dip the eggplant in the flour, shaking off any excess. Then dip the eggplant in the egg. Last, dip the eggplant in the panko. Place the dredged eggplant on a second baking sheet or cutting board, and repeat with the remaining eggplant.

Preheat the oven to 400°F.

Heat the olive oil in a large skillet or Dutch oven over medium-high heat. The oil should be ¼ inch deep. Once the oil begins to shimmer, add the eggplant

Continued on next page

in batches and fry until golden brown, 2 to 3 minutes. Flip the eggplant and continue to cook until the other side is golden brown, 2 more minutes. Clean your cutting board or rimmed baking sheet and line with dry paper towels. Transfer the eggplant to the clean paper towel–lined surface. Repeat with the remaining eggplant, adding more oil as necessary.

Spread ¼ of the tomato sauce in the bottom of a 9×13-inch baking dish. Top with a layer of eggplant. Sprinkle ½ cup of the Parmesan over the eggplant. Repeat with the remaining eggplant, sauce, and Parmesan, creating three layers total. Make sure the top layer is completely covered with sauce. Top with the mozzarella slices and bake for 50 to 55 minutes, until the mozzarella is golden and bubbling.

Let the eggplant Parmesan cool for at least 10 minutes before serving. Eggplant Parmesan can be covered and stored in the refrigerator for up to 3 days, or frozen for up to 3 months.

I love making a double batch of this sauce, so that I can use the other half for the Saucy Tomatoes and Eggs (page 217). Shave Parmesan on the Shaved Zucchini with Bagna Cauda (page 61), dust over the Kale with Lemon and Parmesan (page 95), or pile high on the Creamy Preserved Lemon Pasta (page 109).

Root Vegetable Pot Pie

Serves 4 to 6

This hearty vegetable pot pie is good year-round, but I crave it often when the temperature drops. I'm into a double crust here because I like a high filling-to-crust ratio, but you could totally cut the crust recipe in half and only do the top part if that's your thing. If you want to save even more time, place a sheet of rolled-out puff pastry on top, brush with egg wash, and bake until golden brown.

If you choose to make a double crust (and I hope you will), here are a few things to keep in mind. Like with all pies, you can make the dough up to three days in advance (and keep it in the refrigerator). The longer you let the dough hydrate (chill), the easier it'll be to roll out. The filling should be completely cool before you add it—that means no more steam coming off the top—or the butter in the crust will melt, making it nearly impossible to crimp the crusts together. While the filling cools, roll out the dough and store it on a baking sheet in the refrigerator while you wait.

This is a great recipe to use any of your other favorite root vegetables, like parsnips, radishes, sweet potatoes, fennel, and rutabaga. Just make sure you have roughly six cups of vegetables on hand.

INGREDIENTS

Crust

2½ cups all-purpose flour, plus more for dusting

1 teaspoon kosher salt

1 teaspoon freshly ground black pepper

1 cup (2 sticks) unsalted butter, cold and cubed

4 to 6 tablespoons ice water

Filling

4 tablespoons unsalted butter

1 large yellow onion, finely chopped

4 medium carrots, sliced into ¼-inch pieces on the bias

3 celery stalks, thinly sliced

2 teaspoons kosher salt, divided

4 garlic cloves, minced

2 teaspoons thyme leaves, finely chopped

1 medium celery root, peeled and diced

DIRECTIONS

Make the crust: In the bowl of a food processor, add the flour, salt, and pepper, and pulse three times to combine. Add the butter and pulse to make pieces the size of lima beans. Don't overmix: the bigger the pieces of butter, the flakier the dough will be.

Slowly add the water, 1 tablespoon at a time, until the dough just comes together. It may seem dry at first, but keep pulsing and the dough will come together. Transfer the dough to the countertop and form into two equal disks. Wrap in plastic wrap and refrigerate for at least 1 hour, or up to 3 days.

Preheat the oven to 400°F.

Make the filling: In a large Dutch oven or large pan, melt the butter over medium-high heat. Once melted, add the onion, carrots, and celery and cook, stirring occasionally, until the onion is translucent and the vegetables soften, about 10 minutes. Season with 1 teaspoon of salt.

Add the garlic and thyme and cook until fragrant, stirring occasionally, about 1 minute.

Add the celery root, turnips, and potatoes and stir to combine. Season with the remaining 1 teaspoon of salt and the pepper and cook, stirring occasionally, until the vegetables are just fork-tender, about 10 minutes.

2 medium turnips, scrubbed
and diced
2 Yukon Gold potatoes,
scrubbed and diced
1 teaspoon freshly ground
black pepper
¼ cup all-purpose flour
2 cups vegetable or chicken
stock
2 tablespoons heavy cream

Increase the heat to high and add the flour, stirring until the vegetables are well coated. Cook until the flour is golden brown and no longer raw, about 2 minutes.

Reduce the heat to medium and add the stock, scraping up any brown bits on the bottom of the pot. Cook, stirring occasionally, until the sauce has thickened, about 10 minutes. Remove the pot from the heat and let the mixture cool until no more steam comes off the top, at least 30 minutes, before filling the pie.

On a lightly floured surface, roll out one disk of dough into a circle ⅛ inch thick and 12 inches in diameter. If the dough cracks, simply push it back together. Transfer to a 9-inch pie plate, letting the excess dough hang over the sides. Chill the pie dough while rolling out the other piece.

Roll the second dough disk into a circle ⅛ to ¼ inch thick and 10 inches in diameter and store on a baking sheet in the refrigerator until the filling has cooled.

Fill the pie shell with the vegetable mixture and smooth the top with a spatula. Place the second circle of dough over the filling and trim the edges to be equal in diameter with the first. Crimp the edges. Cut a few slits in the top of the dough to release steam as the pie bakes. Brush the top with the heavy cream.

Set the pie plate on a rimmed baking sheet to catch any drippings and bake until the top is golden brown, about 1 hour.

Let the pie cool for at least 20 minutes before slicing and serving. The pot pie can be covered and stored in the refrigerator for up to 3 days.

Note: If you don't have a food processor, you can make the crust by hand. In a large bowl, whisk the flour, salt, and pepper to combine. Add the butter and use your hands to press the butter into the flour, until the size of lima beans. Add the ice water 1 tablespoon at a time and use your hands to combine, lightly kneading until the dough sticks together.

Don't throw away your pie dough scraps! Instead make Cheesy Pie Dough Crackers (page 31). Any extra carrots in the bunch can be used for Lentil Soup with Parsley (page 117). Make use of the other celery stalks with the Celery Salad with Walnuts and Pecorino (page 63) or the Tuna and White Bean Salad (page 175). Yukon Golds can be swapped for fingerlings in the Fingerling Potato and Leek Top Frittata (page 215). Use the rest of the thyme from this bunch in the Marinated Ricotta Salata with Cracked Spices (page 333), Butter-Basted Lamb Chops (page 155), Chicken Stock (page 234), or White Wine Braised Leeks (page 75). The rest of the bunch of turnips can be saved for the Roasted Radishes and Turnips with Brown Butter Caper Sauce (page 91) or Quick Pickled Vegetables (page 229). Use up heavy cream with the Creamy Preserved Lemon Pasta (page 109), Buttermilk Shortcakes with Roasted Strawberries (page 181), Banana Tarte Tatin (page 187), Orange Meringue Semifreddo (page 189), or Ice Cream Sundae (page 203).

Roasted Radishes and Turnips with Brown Butter Caper Sauce

Serves 4

I love root vegetables and buy a lot of them, so I often have some that have stuck around for too long in the fridge. I use them sliced thinly on salad, or arranged next to a swoop of salty butter on a cheese spread, but when I've exhausted those options for the week, I turn to this recipe. Eaten raw, radishes and turnips have a peppery, fresh flavor. But roasted, they become almost sweet and creamy. You could eat them as is, but I like to finish them off with a nutty brown butter sauce.

This recipe calls for both the root of these vegetables and their tops. Seriously, don't toss the tops! Most radish tops will have to be washed a few times to remove any grit, but the extra step is worth it. When the tops are roasted they become crispy, almost chiplike. Don't worry about any spiky leaves—they'll melt away once roasted.

INGREDIENTS

1 bunch radishes, halved
1 bunch baby turnips, halved, or 2 medium turnips, cut into eighths
¼ cup olive oil
1 teaspoon kosher salt
3 tablespoons unsalted butter
1 teaspoon Dijon mustard
Juice of ½ lemon
2 tablespoons finely chopped parsley
1 tablespoon capers, drained and rinsed, roughly chopped

DIRECTIONS

Preheat the oven to 400°F.

Place the radishes and turnips on a rimmed baking sheet and drizzle with the olive oil and sprinkle with the salt, using your hands to toss to coat.

Roast the radishes and turnips until the roots are golden brown and fork-tender and the greens are crispy, about 25 minutes. Radishes and turnips can be stored in a sealed container in the refrigerator for up to 3 days, although the tops will no longer be crispy.

Meanwhile, add the butter to a small saucepan over medium-high heat, twirling the pan occasionally until the butter melts and foams. Reduce the heat to low and continue cooking until the butter turns golden brown and smells nutty, 2 to 3 minutes. Remove the pan from the heat and cool for at least 5 minutes before using.

Add the Dijon, lemon juice, parsley, and capers to the brown butter and whisk to combine. Pour the brown butter sauce over the radishes and turnips, and serve immediately.

Parsley can be used in the Squash with Herby Salsa Verde (page 101), Greens Skillet Pie (page 83), Bucatini with Tuna and Olives (page 107), Spicy Brothy Bacony Beans (page 115), Crispy Chicken Thighs with Chickpeas and Olives (page 133), Herby Chicken Salad (page 134), or Red Wine Braised Short Rib Ragout (page 137). Serve any leftover radishes with the Aioli (page 23), with Whipped Feta and Charred Scallion Dip (page 35), on top of the Chilled Green Soup (page 97), or sliced in the Green Goddess Salad (page 53). Turnips add great flavor in the Root Vegetable Pot Pie (page 88).

Mashed Sweet Potatoes with Honey Butter and Pickled Chilies

Serves 4

Sometimes I forget how much I like sweet potatoes—and then I'll have them again and remember how very good they are. I prefer roasting to boiling sweet potatoes, as they take on a more concentrated flavor in the oven as their natural sugars caramelize. To balance that sweetness, I top the potatoes with zesty lime honey butter, spicy pickled Fresno chilies, and a handful of scallions.

This mash is on the chunky side, so if you prefer it smoother, pulse the cooked sweet potatoes in a food processor until you reach your desired consistency. Save extra pickled chilies to layer on sandwiches or chop to use in grain bowls or, of course, on eggs.

INGREDIENTS

Quick Pickled Fresno Chilies
½ cup water
¾ cup apple cider vinegar
2 teaspoons kosher salt
1 tablespoon light brown sugar
¼ teaspoon black peppercorns
2 garlic cloves, crushed
2 Fresno chilies, thinly sliced

Lime Honey Butter
½ cup (1 stick) unsalted butter, at room temperature
Zest of 1 lime
Juice of ½ lime
2 teaspoons honey

4 medium sweet potatoes, washed
1 tablespoon olive oil
½ teaspoon kosher salt
3 scallions, white and light green parts thinly sliced

DIRECTIONS

Make the pickled Fresno chilies: In a small pot, add the water, vinegar, salt, brown sugar, peppercorns, and garlic and bring to a boil over high heat, whisking until the sugar dissolves. Remove the pot from the heat and add the sliced chilies. Let cool to room temperature for at least 1 hour. Use immediately or store in a sealed container in the refrigerator for up to 2 weeks.

Make the honey butter: Add the butter to a small bowl along with the lime zest and juice, and honey, and use a fork to combine.

Preheat the oven to 400°F.

Make the sweet potatoes: Use a fork to poke holes all over the sweet potatoes. Place the potatoes on a rimmed baking sheet and rub with the olive oil. This will help steam release as the potatoes cook.

Bake the potatoes until easily pierced with a knife, about 1 hour. Let the potatoes cool to room temperature, then transfer them to a cutting board and slice them in half lengthwise. Use a spoon to scoop out the flesh of the potatoes and transfer to a large bowl. Use a potato masher to mash the sweet potatoes until chunky.

Add 6 tablespoons of the honey butter and the salt to the potatoes and stir to combine. Top the potatoes with the remaining 2 tablespoons of honey butter, along with the scallions, and 1 tablespoon of the pickled Fresno chilies. The mashed sweet potatoes can be stored in a sealed container in the refrigerator for up to 5 days. Wait until just before serving to top with the scallions and pickled Fresno chilies.

Don't toss the sweet potato skins! Save them to make one of my favorite snacks, Crispy Sweet Potato Skins with Crème Fraîche (page 47). Use the rest of the scallions for Herby Chicken Salad (page 134).

Charred Cauliflower with Zhoug and Pine Nuts

Serves 2 to 4

I know it sounds boring to season cauliflower—or just about anything—with only salt and pepper, but the trick here is in how it's prepared. First, cauliflower gets roasted in a generous amount of olive oil and becomes charred . . . with no salt. Salting cauliflower before roasting draws out the moisture, rendering it more soft than browned. Next comes salt and pepper. It's so good you'll be tempted to eat it straight from the tray. But wait! I like to slather the cauliflower in zhoug (sometimes spelled *zhug*), a spicy Yemeni condiment, and shower it with creamy pine nuts. Variations of zhoug can be found all over the Middle East—there's green, red, and even smoked versions–but all pack a punch. My version is made with cilantro, jalapeños, garlic, and spices. Suddenly salt and pepper cauliflower doesn't seem so boring after all.

INGREDIENTS

Cauliflower

1 head cauliflower, florets removed, tender stalk thinly sliced
¼ cup olive oil
1 teaspoon kosher salt
1 teaspoon freshly ground black pepper
2 tablespoons pine nuts

Zhoug

2 cups (1 bunch) roughly chopped cilantro leaves and stems
2 jalapeño, sliced
3 garlic cloves, roughly chopped
1 teaspoon kosher salt
1 teaspoon ground cumin
½ teaspoon ground cardamom
Juice of 1 lemon
¼ cup olive oil

DIRECTIONS

Preheat the oven to 400°F.

Make the cauliflower: Place the cauliflower florets on a baking sheet, drizzle with the olive oil, and using your hands, toss until well coated. Roast until charred on one side, about 25 minutes. Use a spatula to flip the florets and continue roasting until the cauliflower is easily pierced with a knife and charred all over, about 15 minutes more.

Make the zhoug: While the cauliflower is roasting, make the zhoug. In the bowl of a food processor, add the cilantro, jalapeños, garlic, salt, cumin, cardamom, and lemon juice, and pulse until combined. With the motor running, pour in the olive oil until smooth. The zhoug lasts in a sealed container in the refrigerator for up to 1 week.

Transfer the cauliflower to a serving platter and season with the salt and pepper and toss to combine. Top with the zhoug and sprinkle with the pine nuts. The cauliflower can be stored in a sealed container in the refrigerator for up to 3 days.

Roast an extra batch of cauliflower and use it for the Cauliflower and Cheddar Strata (page 221).

Kale with Lemon and Parmesan

Serves 2 to 4

My best friend from college introduced me to massaged kale salads (with lots of lemon and garlic). I was so obsessed with it that we ate this salad at least twice a week for two years. This recipe feels simultanesouly like I'm being a beacon of health and an indulgent treat, thanks to a showering of Parmesan. My favorite part? You can make it in under five minutes.

I usually keep the stems on if I'm cooking kale, but when it's raw it's better to remove them (and save them for quick pickling (page 227). Raw kale stems are pretty fibrous and hard to digest.

INGREDIENTS

2 garlic cloves, grated

Zest and juice of 1 lemon, divided

¼ teaspoon kosher salt

2 tablespoons olive oil

1 bunch lacinato kale, stems removed, leaves roughly torn

Flaky sea salt

¼ cup grated Parmesan

DIRECTIONS

Add the garlic, lemon zest, salt, and olive oil to a large bowl.

Place the kale leaves in the bowl and use your hands to massage the kale for 1 to 2 minutes, until the kale has reduced to half the size and no longer feels fibrous to the touch.

Drizzle the lemon juice over the kale and toss until just combined. Sprinkle with flaky sea salt. Top with the grated Parmesan. The kale salad is best served within an hour of being massaged.

Parmesan is pricey, so I try to squeeze every last bit of flavor out of it. Add the rind to the Spicy Brothy Bacony Beans (page 115), Chicken Stock (page 234), Corn Stock (page 235), or Parmesan Broth (page 237).

Chilled Green Soup

Serves 2 to 4

When it's too hot to think about turning on the stove, and I'm craving something healthy(ish), I make this chilled green soup. It takes a cue from gazpacho and begins in a similar way: a piece of soaked bread that thickens the soup without altering the flavor. Peppery arugula and basil are then added, and later mellowed with yogurt—which also adds creaminess—resulting in a light, herbaceous soup. Top it with crispy bread crumbs and sliced radishes for some crunch.

INGREDIENTS

Chilled Green Soup

1 slice bread, crusts removed

1 green bell pepper, seeded and roughly chopped

1 English cucumber, peeled, seeded, roughly chopped

2 cups arugula

½ cup basil leaves

1 medium shallot, roughly chopped

2 garlic cloves

¼ cup olive oil

½ cup hot water

¼ cup plain whole milk yogurt

2 teaspoons kosher salt

3 teaspoons sherry vinegar

2 radishes, thinly sliced

Crispy Bread Crumbs

2 tablespoons olive oil

½ cup panko or homemade bread crumbs

¼ teaspoon kosher salt

2 radishes, thinly sliced, to serve

DIRECTIONS

Make the soup: Run the bread under cold water, then use your hands to squeeze out the excess water. Place the bread in the bowl of the food processor.

Add the bell pepper, cucumber, arugula, basil, shallot, garlic, olive oil, water, yogurt, salt, and vinegar to a blender, and blend until smooth.

Transfer the soup to a sealable container and chill in the refrigerator for at least 8 hours, and up to 2 days. The longer the soup sits, the more flavorful it will become.

Make the crispy bread crumbs: Heat the olive oil in a medium pan over medium-high heat. Once the oil begins to shimmer, add the panko and cook, stirring often, until golden brown, about 2 minutes. Transfer the bread crumbs to a paper towel–lined plate and season with the salt.

Serve the soup topped with the crispy bread crumbs and the radish slices.

Use the rest of the yogurt for the Yogurt Chive Flatbread (page 37) or Green Goddess Salad (page 53). Since this recipe calls for only one slice of bread, the remaining loaf can be used in the Cauliflower and Cheddar Strata (page 221); Panzanella with Tomatoes, Melon, and Pickled Mustard Seeds (page 51); or Homemade Bread Crumbs (page 239). Arugula can be added to the Everyday Green Salad (page 56), or the Greens Skillet Pie (page 83). Extra basil can be used in the carrot top pesto (page 113), Charred Corn and Burrata (page 79), Crispy Rice Salad (page 121), or Herby Chicken Salad (page 134). Basil and crispy panko can be saved for the Squash with Herby Salsa Verde (page 101). Serve extra radishes with the Aioli (page 23), or Whipped Feta and Charred Scallion Dip (page 35).

Corn Soup with Garlic Chips

Serves 4

At the peak of summer when sweet corn is in season, I try to use it in as many preparations as possible. Enter this (vegan!) spiced corn soup, which gets a kick from curry powder and lime juice. My chef friend Karlee taught me a trick a few years back: add a bit of rice to soup to thicken it. The result is a creamy texture without adding any dairy. I like topping this soup with garlic chips, which offer a mellowed garlicky flavor and a whole lot of crunch.

A few notes here: If fresh corn isn't in season, use six cups of frozen, thawed corn. If fresh corn is in season, I use corn cobs to make corn stock, which makes this soup extra flavorful. But if you're short on time or just not into the extra step, vegetable stock will work in its place. If you're making your own corn stock, reserve the corn cobs and refer to page 235 for the recipe.

INGREDIENTS

Corn Soup

2 tablespoons olive oil, plus more for serving
1 yellow onion, finely chopped
2 celery stalks, thinly sliced
3 garlic cloves, minced
6 medium ears of corn, kernels removed and reserved
1½ teaspoons kosher salt
1 tablespoon curry powder
1 teaspoon turmeric
1 teaspoon paprika
⅓ cup arborio or short grain white rice
6 cups Corn Stock or vegetable stock
Juice of 1 lime
¼ cup cilantro leaves, roughly torn, to serve

Garlic Chips

2 tablespoons grapeseed oil
4 garlic cloves, thinly sliced
⅛ teaspoon kosher salt

DIRECTIONS

Make the corn soup: Heat the olive oil in a Dutch oven or large pot over medium-high heat. Once the oil begins to shimmer, add the onion and celery and cook, stirring occasionally, until lightly browned, 7 to 8 minutes.

Add the garlic and cook until fragrant, about 1 minute. Add the corn, salt, curry powder, turmeric, and paprika and cook, stirring often, until the spices are toasted and fragrant, about 3 minutes.

Add the rice and stir to combine.

Add the stock and bring to a boil. Reduce the heat to medium-low and simmer until the rice is cooked through and the soup is thickened, about 20 minutes.

Transfer the soup to a blender or food processor and pulse until smooth. (A blender will result in a smoother soup.) Transfer the soup back to the pot and return to a simmer. Before serving, add the lime juice and stir to combine. The soup can be stored in a sealed container in the refrigerator for up to 3 days, or frozen for up to 3 months.

Make the garlic chips: Heat the grapeseed oil in a medium skillet over high heat. Once the oil begins to shimmer, add the garlic and immediately turn the heat to low. Cook, stirring constantly, until golden brown, about 1 minute. Transfer the garlic to a paper towel–lined plate and sprinkle with the salt. The garlic chips can be stored in a sealed container at room temperature for up to 1 week.

Serve the soup with a few cilantro leaves, garlic chips, and a drizzle of olive oil.

I don't need to tell you to save rice, but Weeknight Rice (page 118) is really worth making, as is the Crispy Rice Salad (page 121). The California Citrus Salad (page 55), Carrot Ribbon Salad (page 59), Charred Cauliflower with Zhoug and Pine Nuts (page 93), Whole Red Snapper with Cilantro and Lime (page 169), and Baja-Style Fish Tacos (page 171) are all great ways to use up cilantro. Save celery for the Root Vegetable Pot Pie (page 88).

Squash with Herby Salsa Verde

Serves 4 to 6

This is a far cry from the brown sugar and butternut squash nineties kids remember. I wanted a recipe that played off, rather than on, the vegetable's natural sweetness. Now I reach for this herby green sauce to complement the sweetness of the squash.

INGREDIENTS

Squash
2 acorn squash
2 tablespoons olive oil
1½ teaspoons kosher salt
1½ teaspoons freshly ground
  black pepper

Herby Salsa Verde
1 cup (½ bunch) cilantro,
  leaves and stems roughly
  chopped
1 cup (½ bunch) parsley,
  leaves and stems roughly
  chopped
½ cup basil leaves
½ cup mint leaves
1 large shallot, roughly
  chopped
2 tablespoons capers,
  drained and rinsed
½ cup plus 1 tablespoon
  olive oil
2 tablespoons sherry vinegar
½ teaspoon kosher salt
¼ teaspoon freshly ground
  black pepper
½ teaspoon crushed red
  pepper flakes, optional
2 teaspoons honey

Crispy Bread Crumbs
2 tablespoons olive oil
½ cup panko or homemade
  bread crumbs (page 239)
¼ teaspoon kosher salt

DIRECTIONS

Preheat the oven to 400°F.

Make the squash: On a cutting board, quarter the squash. Use a large spoon to remove the seeds and reserve for a later use. Place the squash on a rimmed baking sheet cut side up, drizzle with the olive oil, and season with salt and pepper, using your hands to coat them all over. Roast until easily pierced with a knife, about 1 hour.

Make the herby salsa verde: In the bowl of a food processor, add the cilantro, parsley, basil, mint, shallot, and capers, and blend until roughly chopped. Add the olive oil and blend until just combined. Add the vinegar, salt, black pepper, red pepper flakes, and honey and pulse to combine. The salsa verde can be stored in a sealed container in the refrigerator for up to 3 days. Makes 1 cup.

Make the crispy bread crumbs: Heat the olive oil in a medium pan over medium-high heat. Once the oil begins to shimmer, add the panko and cook, stirring often, until golden brown, about 2 minutes. Transfer the bread crumbs to a paper towel–lined plate and season with the salt.

Serve the squash topped with the herby salsa verde and crispy bread crumbs. The squash can be stored separately from the bread crumbs and herby salsa verde in a sealed container in the refrigerator for up to 2 days.

Save the seeds for Crunchy Squash Seeds (page 39). Save cilantro for the California Citrus Salad (page 55), Carrot Ribbon Salad (page 59), Charred Cauliflower with Zhoug and Pine Nuts (page 93), and Baja-Style Fish Tacos (page 171). Use parsley for the Spicy Brothy Bacony Beans (page 115), Farro with Mushrooms (page 123), Crispy Chicken Thighs with Chickpeas and Olives (page 133), Herby Chicken Salad (page 134), Red Wine Braised Short Rib Ragout (page 137), or the Tuna and White Bean Salad (page 175). Basil gets added to the Chilled Green Soup (page 97), Orechiette with Carrot Top Pesto and Peas (page 113), and Curried Mussels with Basil (page 166). Mint is key for the Crispy Rice Salad (page 121), or Israeli Couscous with Herbs (page 125).

PASTA, BEANS, AND GRAINS

Pasta with Tomato Confit and Ricotta

Bucatini with Tuna and Olives

Creamy Preserved Lemon Pasta

Garlic Confit Mac and Cheese

Orecchiette with Carrot Top Pesto and Peas

Spicy Brothy Bacony Beans

Lentil Soup with Parsley

Weeknight Rice

Creamy Gruyère Polenta

Crispy Rice Salad

Farro with Mushrooms

Israeli Couscous with Herbs

Pasta with Tomato Confit and Ricotta

Serves 4

Confit is a French technique to preserve food by slowly cooking it in fat. While this method works particularly well for poultry, it isn't just for (most famously) duck—you can also preserve vegetables like eggplant, carrots, beans, and my favorite, tomatoes.

I love tomato confit on just about everything—topped on pizza, piled high on charred sourdough, swirled in with creamy polenta—but I find it's particularly good mixed into pasta with heaps of ricotta. It's one of my favorite weeknight meals when I have an abundance of tomatoes on the counter that have started to wither or have just passed their peak flavor—this is a great way to resurrect them.

INGREDIENTS
6 cups (3 pints) cherry tomatoes
¾ cup olive oil
1½ teaspoons kosher salt
1 teaspoon freshly ground black pepper
½ teaspoon crushed red pepper flakes
3 garlic cloves, lightly smashed
3 sprigs rosemary
1 pound short pasta of choice, such as gemelli, garganelli, or penne
1 container (15 ounces) whole milk ricotta

DIRECTIONS
Preheat the oven to 300°F.

Place the tomatoes, olive oil, salt, black pepper, red pepper flakes, garlic, and rosemary on a rimmed baking sheet and, with your hands, toss to combine.

Roast until the tomatoes have softened and burst, about 1½ hours. Remove the rosemary and discard. Let the tomatoes cool in the oil for at least 10 minutes before serving. Alternatively, the tomatoes and oil can be cooled to room temperature, then transferred to a sealable container and stored in the refrigerator for up to 1 week.

Cook the pasta in a large pot of salted water according to package instructions until al dente. Drain the pasta in a colander and shake off any excess water. Transfer the pasta to a large serving bowl and add the tomato confit and ¼ cup of the oil from the pan. Reserve the remaining oil for a later use, such as vinaigrettes, drizzling over grain bowls, or frying eggs.

Top with dollops of the ricotta before serving.

Bucatini with Tuna and Olives

Serves 2 to 4

A few summers ago a group of friends and I planned and saved for months to rent a house in Mallorca. Our house was perched in the hillside of Deia, a town made up of stone houses with kelly green and cornflower blue shutters, winding cobblestone streets lined with oleander trees, and one lone grocery store with well-stocked shelves but sporadic hours. When we stopped by, we made sure to purchase pantry staples that could be transformed into multiple meals. We ate this pasta at the end of long days in the sun when a quick dinner was all I had energy to make. Long after that vacation ended, it's become a go-to for all of us.

I like using tuna packed in oil, which has more flavor, but if you've only got water-packed, that's fine—just add another tablespoon of olive oil to the pasta before serving. If you want to make it vegetarian, swap the tuna for one can of drained and rinsed white beans. It's just as satisfying.

INGREDIENTS

½ pound bucatini or long pasta of choice

3 tablespoons olive oil

2 garlic cloves, grated

½ teaspoon crushed red pepper flakes

1 teaspoon kosher salt

½ teaspoon freshly ground black pepper

½ cup pitted Castelvetrano olives, roughly chopped

1 tablespoon capers, drained and rinsed

Zest and juice of 1 lemon

2 cans (5 ounces each) olive oil–packed tuna, drained

¼ cup parsley leaves, chopped

DIRECTIONS

Cook the bucatini in a large pot of salted water according to package instructions until al dente. Drain the pasta in a colander and shake off any excess water.

Meanwhile, in a large bowl, add the olive oil, garlic, red pepper flakes, salt, black pepper, olives, capers, lemon zest, and tuna, and stir until combined.

Add the drained pasta, lemon juice, and parsley, and toss until well combined.

The Crispy Chicken Thighs with Chickpeas and Olives (page 133) are a great way to use those Castelvetrano olives, as is the Mixed Olive Tapenade (page 44). Add parsley to the Squash with Herby Salsa Verde (page 101), Greens Skillet Pie (page 83), Roasted Radishes and Turnips with Brown Butter Caper Sauce (page 91), Spicy Brothy Bacony Beans (page 115), Herby Chicken Salad (page 134), or Red Wine Braised Short Rib Ragout (page 137).

Creamy Preserved Lemon Pasta

Serves 2 to 4

This supremely simple pasta comes together in minutes and relies on lemon in two ways. Thinly sliced preserved lemons and lemon zest are first steeped in heavy cream. Preserved lemons add a more concentrated, almost briny lemon flavor, while the zest adds a bright lemon flavor. Then Parmesan and starchy pasta water are added, which turns this mixture into a zesty, silky sauce. The best part is the whole thing comes together in a matter of minutes, making it an ideal weeknight meal.

Make sure you have your ingredients measured out before you begin—this sauce can go from creamy to lumpy quickly. Use the fine side of a box grater to prepare the Parmesan. A rasp grater will grate the cheese too finely, which makes it stick together rather than melt evenly into the sauce. I like mafaldine for its ruffled edges that sauce easily clings to, but any long pasta, like spaghetti or bucatini, will work here.

INGREDIENTS

12 ounces mafaldine or any long pasta

4 tablespoons unsalted butter

2 garlic cloves, grated

1 cup heavy cream

Zest of 1 lemon

1 preserved lemon, thinly sliced

¼ teaspoon kosher salt

1 teaspoon freshly ground black pepper, plus more to serve

1 cup grated Parmesan, plus more to serve

DIRECTIONS

Cook the mafaldine in a large pot of salted water according to package instructions until 1 minute shy of al dente. Reserve ½ cup of the pasta water, then drain the pasta through a colander.

Add the butter to a large pan over medium-high heat. Once the butter melts, add the garlic and cook for about 30 seconds, or until fragrant. Add the cream, lemon zest, and preserved lemon and bring to a simmer. Reduce the heat to medium-low and cook until slightly thickened and reduced by one-fourth, 3 to 4 minutes. Add the salt and pepper and stir to combine.

Add the drained pasta, the ½ cup of reserved pasta water, and the grated Parmesan and quickly toss with tongs until the sauce fully coats the pasta, 1 to 2 minutes.

Top with more pepper and grated Parmesan. Serve immediately.

See Preserved Lemons (page 227), then use them here and in the Israeli Couscous with Herbs (page 125). Save the Parmesan rind for Chicken Stock (page 234), Parmesan Broth (page 237), or Spicy Brothy Bacony Beans (page 115). Use up heavy cream in the Root Vegetable Pot Pie (page 88), Buttermilk Shortcakes with Roasted Strawberries (page 181), Banana Tarte Tatin (page 187), Orange Meringue Semifreddo (page 189), or Ice Cream Sundae (page 203).

Garlic Confit Mac and Cheese

Serves 6 to 8

My mom—raised in the Netherlands with an adventurous palate—was never into making what she called "kid" food. You know, stuff you would see on a kids' menu, like hot dogs, chicken tenders, and butter noodles. Since we didn't eat it at home, I didn't often crave it . . . *except* for mac and cheese, which is arguably the ultimate kid food. Every winter she'd cave and make a big tray with three types of cheeses in the sauce, topped with a layer of buttery, golden-brown bread crumbs.

My version is a riff on hers. I use three cheeses, too: a mix of cheddar and Gruyère for a flavor that's both sharp and nutty, and Fontina for a texture that's extra melty. I also add garlic confit, which delivers a mellow, almost sweet garlic flavor throughout. If you don't have the time for that step, skip it and this recipe still makes a great mac and cheese.

I prefer grating the cheese myself, since preshredded cheese can sometimes contain preservatives that can clump, rather than melt, in the sauce. Opt for a box grater (or food processor) that does the work in a matter of minutes. If you have the willpower to resist eating a whole tray of mac and cheese within twenty-four hours (I don't), you could portion it out after baking and store it in the freezer for up to three months.

INGREDIENTS

Garlic Confit
1 cup extra-virgin olive oil
1 head garlic, peeled

Mac and Cheese
1 pound shells, elbows, or cavatappi pasta
2½ tablespoons unsalted butter, divided
1 cup homemade bread crumbs or panko
1½ teaspoons kosher salt, divided
2 tablespoons all-purpose flour
2 cups whole milk
½ teaspoon freshly ground black pepper
1 teaspoon smoked paprika
3 cups (12 ounces) grated white cheddar cheese
2 cups (8 ounces) grated Gruyère cheese
2 cups (8 ounces) grated Fontina cheese

DIRECTIONS

Make the garlic confit: In a small pot, heat the olive oil for 5 minutes over low heat.

Add the garlic and simmer for about 30 minutes, or until the garlic can be easily pierced with a knife. Reserve ¼ cup of the garlic oil. Remove four cloves of garlic and smash into a paste. Store the remaining garlic oil and cloves in a sealed container for up to 2 weeks at room temperature. The reserved garlic oil and cloves can be used for vinaigrettes, roasting vegetables, or drizzled over toast.

Make the mac and cheese: Cook the pasta in a large pot of salted water according to package instructions until a little below al dente. Drain the pasta and set aside.

Preheat the oven to 350°F. Grease a 9x13-inch baking dish with the ½ tablespoon of butter.

Heat 3 tablespoons of the reserved garlic oil in a large pan over medium heat. Once the oil begins to shimmer, add the bread crumbs and stir for about 4 minutes, or until golden brown. Transfer the bread crumbs to a paper towel–lined plate and season with the ½ teaspoon of salt.

Continued on next page

In a large pot, melt the remaining 2 tablespoons of butter over medium-high heat. Add the flour and whisk for about 2 minutes, or until golden brown.

Add the milk, mashed garlic, the remaining 1 teaspoon of salt, the pepper, and paprika. Cook, whisking constantly, for about 6 minutes, until thick and creamy.

Add the cheddar, Gruyère, and Fontina, stir until melted, about 1 minute. Add the pasta and stir to coat well.

Transfer the pasta to the prepared baking dish. Sprinkle the bread crumbs in an even layer over the top.

Bake until the pasta is bubbling and the bread crumbs are golden brown, about 50 minutes. Let cool for at least 10 minutes before serving. The mac and cheese lasts for up to 4 days covered in the refrigerator, or for 3 months in a sealed container in the freezer.

If you have extra cheese, use the Gruyère in the Creamy Gruyère Polenta (page 119), the cheddar in the Cauliflower and Cheddar Strata (page 221), or see This is How You Make a Cheese Plate (page 27).

Orecchiette with Carrot Top Pesto and Peas

Serves 4

Pesto is perhaps the most obvious choice for using up carrot tops, but it's popular for a reason. Blitzed with basil, this version takes on a more earthy flavor than the standard variety.

When using carrot tops, make sure to thoroughly wash them in a salad spinner to remove any lingering grit. Save the stems, which are too tough for pesto, for the next time you make Chicken Stock (page 234).

INGREDIENTS

1 cup carrot tops, stems reserved for a later use, roughly chopped

3 cups loosely packed basil

¼ cup pine nuts

1 large garlic clove, grated

1 cup (4 ounces) grated Parmesan

½ teaspoon kosher salt

¼ teaspoon freshly ground black pepper

½ cup olive oil

1 pound orecchiette or short pasta of choice

1 package (10 ounces) frozen peas

DIRECTIONS

In the bowl of a food processor, add the carrot tops, basil, pine nuts, garlic, Parmesan, salt, and pepper, and pulse until combined. With the motor running, add the olive oil and process until smooth. Carrot top pesto can be stored in the refrigerator in a sealed container for up to 1 week.

Boil the pasta in a large pot of salted water according to package instructions until 2 minutes shy of al dente. Add the peas and continue cooking until the pasta is al dente. Reserve ¼ cup of pasta water, then drain the pasta and peas through a colander. Transfer the pasta and the peas to a serving bowl. Add the pesto and reserved pasta water and quickly stir to combine until well coated.

Using up carrots is the easy part. Try the Carrot Ribbon Salad (page 59), Lentil Soup with Parsley (page 117), Red Wine Braised Short Rib Ragout (page 137), or Spatchcock Paprika Chicken with Carrots and Onions (page 129). Pine nuts are pricey, so I use them sparingly, but I think they really add something to the Charred Cauliflower with Zhoug and Pine Nuts (page 93).

Spicy Brothy Bacony Beans

Serves 4 to 6

It took me years to figure out how to make a good pot of beans. Time is the secret ingredient. If your beans aren't tender enough, just keep cooking them. If the liquid evaporates, add a splash of water or stock until the beans are covered and just keep cooking them some more. Taste a few; when they're soft and taste almost creamy, they're ready. Serve the beans with some crusty bread, pile them on a taco, spooned over rice, or eat them straight from the pot like I do.

The real joy of dried beans is much the same as homemade stock: you can make them to suit your tastes. I call for bacon here, but if you don't have it (or want a vegetarian option), leave it out. Fennel stalks, dried chilies, and herbs like thyme and parsley are great flavor boosters.

When it comes to the beans themselves, I'm partial to cranberry beans, but this recipe works with nearly any type—pinto, great northern beans, black beans, even chickpeas. I like to soak my beans overnight, which speeds up the cooking time the next day, but you don't have to; just know that they'll take a bit longer once on the stove.

INGREDIENTS

1 pound dried cranberry beans or dried beans of choice

4 ounces bacon, cut into ½-inch slices

1 yellow onion, cut into eighths

3 large garlic cloves, lightly smashed

1 medium jalapeño, halved

6 cups Chicken Stock (page 234)

1 Parmesan rind

5 sprigs parsley

2 tablespoons olive oil

Kosher salt, to taste

DIRECTIONS

Pick through the beans, discarding any broken ones or other debris. Place the beans in a large bowl. Fill with cold water to cover the beans by at least 3 inches. Soak the beans at room temperature for 12 hours, or overnight. Drain the beans in a colander, shaking off any excess water.

Heat a large pot or Dutch oven over medium-high heat. Once the pot is hot, add the bacon and cook for about 8 minutes, or until crispy. Remove the bacon with a slotted spoon and transfer to a paper towel–lined plate, leaving the bacon fat in the pot.

Add the onion to the pot and cook for about 6 minutes, stirring occasionally, or until the onion is browned at the edges and beginning to soften. Add the garlic and jalapeño and cook until the garlic is golden and fragrant, about 1 minute.

Add the beans, stock, Parmesan rind, parsley, and olive oil to the pot, making sure the beans are covered by at least 2 inches of stock. If not, add water. Bring to a simmer, then reduce the heat to medium-low, and simmer until the beans begin to soften, about 2 hours. Season with salt and cook until the beans are tender and creamy, about 45 minutes more. Stir in the bacon and taste for seasoning, adding more salt as necessary. The beans can be kept in a sealed container in the refrigerator for up to 1 week, or frozen for up to 3 months.

Save extra bacon for Really Good Meatballs (page 135), or the BLT Salad (page 57). Use parsley in the Bucatini with Tuna and Olives (page 107), Farro with Mushrooms (page 123), Herby Chicken Salad (page 134), or Red Wine Braised Short Rib Ragout (page 137).

Lentil Soup with Parsley

Serves 6

This is based on my mom's lentil soup, which is a beloved winter staple in our house. She got it from her best friend's mother in the 1970s, and she's been making it ever since. I've made this for countless friends over the years, and without fail they ask for the recipe every time—it's that good. The first thing people notice is that there's no crisping the bacon, which leads some to panic that it's not really cooked. But trust me on this one. As the lentils simmer, the bacon slowly renders and flavors the soup. Just before serving, you remove the bacon from the pot, slice it thinly, and then add it back. When you're lucky enough to taste a bite with lentils *and* bacon, the meat literally melts in your mouth. Everyone who has ever tried this lentil soup, even early skeptics, says it's the best they've ever had.

INGREDIENTS

1 pound brown lentils

1 package (12 ounces) sliced bacon

2 tablespoons olive oil

1 large yellow onion, finely chopped

3 medium carrots, finely chopped

3 celery stalks, finely chopped

3 garlic cloves, minced

1 teaspoon freshly ground black pepper

8 cups Chicken Stock (page 234)

1 dried bay leaf

2 bunches parsley, 1 tied with kitchen twine, 1 roughly chopped

1 cup celery leaves, roughly chopped

Flaky sea salt

DIRECTIONS

Place the lentils in a fine mesh sieve and run under cold water. Discard any shriveled lentils or other debris.

On a cutting board, stack the bacon, then tie it together with three pieces of 6-inch kitchen twine.

Heat the olive oil in a large stockpot or Dutch oven over medium-high heat. Once the oil begins to shimmer, add the onion, carrots, and celery, and cook until softened, stirring occasionally, about 10 minutes.

Add the garlic and pepper and cook, stirring often, until fragrant, 1 minute.

Add the lentils and stir to coat with the oil and aromatics. Add the stock, bay leaf, and tied pack of bacon, and bring to a boil over high heat.

Add the tied bunch of parsley and reduce the heat to low. Place the lid on the pot and simmer until the lentils are tender, about 1½ hours.

Discard the bay leaf and parsley. Remove the bacon and untie the string. Finely slice the bacon, then return it back to the pot, stirring to combine.

Before serving, add the chopped parsley and celery leaves and stir once to combine. Top with flaky sea salt to taste. The lentil soup lasts for up to 5 days in a sealed container in the refrigerator, or for up to 3 months in the freezer.

Use extra celery (leaves too!) in the Celery Salad with Walnuts and Pecorino (page 63), Tuna and White Bean Salad (page 175), Corn Soup with Garlic Chips (page 99) or Chicken Stock (page 234). The rest of the carrot bunch can be used in the Red Wine Braised Short Rib Ragout (page 137).

Weeknight Rice

Serves 2 to 4

This shallot and white wine–infused dish is one of my favorite recipes for rice. I serve it with just about everything—seriously. From Black Garlic Butter Salmon with Scallions (page 163) and White Wine Braised Leeks (page 75) to Charred Cauliflower with Zhoug and Pine Nuts (page 93), this rice is the perfect side dish. My friends have gone so far as to call it *the* rice—that's how good it is. These same friends sometimes say that making rice can be daunting, but I think that's only because there's confusion about cooking time. This always works for me: turn the heat all the way down to the lowest setting and simmer for precisely eighteen minutes. You're guaranteed perfect rice every time.

INGREDIENTS

1 tablespoon olive oil
1 medium shallot, roughly chopped
1 cup long grain white rice
¼ cup dry white wine, such as sauvignon blanc
1¼ cups chicken or vegetable stock
Pinch of kosher salt

DIRECTIONS

Heat the olive oil in a small pot over medium-high heat. Add the shallot and cook, stirring frequently, until the shallot softens and turns golden brown, about 2 minutes.

Add the rice and stir to coat in the olive oil and cook until toasted and beginning to turn lightly golden, about 1 minute. Add the wine and stir to combine, cooking until the alcohol has burned off, about 1 minute.

Add the stock and salt and bring to a boil over high heat. Place the lid on the pot and reduce heat to the lowest setting and simmer for 18 minutes.

Remove from the heat and keep the lid on for 5 minutes before serving. If not serving immediately, the rice can be kept in a sealed container for up to 3 days in the refrigerator.

Keep any leftover rice in the fridge for a few days to dry out, then use it in the Crispy Rice Salad (page 121).

Creamy Gruyère Polenta

Serves 4

The key to making really good polenta is patience (like most things in life). Slowly simmer the polenta over low heat, while constantly stirring, to ensure a ridiculously silky texture, no lumps in sight. Serve it like I do with Red Wine Braised Short Rib Ragout (page 137), saucy shrimp, or Tomato Confit (page 105).

INGREDIENTS

4 cups chicken or vegetable stock

1 cup polenta

2 tablespoons butter

½ teaspoon kosher salt

½ teaspoon freshly ground black pepper

1 cup grated Gruyère cheese

DIRECTIONS

Add the stock to a medium pot over medium-high heat and bring to a boil. Add the polenta and whisk until the polenta is smooth and beginning to thicken, about 2 minutes.

Reduce the heat to low and simmer the polenta, whisking often to prevent it from sticking to the bottom, until thickened, about 45 minutes. Add the butter, salt, pepper, and Gruyère, and whisk until the butter and cheese are just melted. The polenta is best served immediately.

This is How You Make a Cheese Plate (page 27) is a great way to use up Gruyère, as is the Garlic Confit Mac and Cheese (page 111).

Crispy Rice Salad

Serves 4 to 6

Sure, you could make fried rice with your leftovers, but have you tried crispy rice? When I lived in Los Angeles, anytime I ordered Laotian food I'd always order nam khao, a Laotian dish traditionally made by frying balls of rice, then breaking them up and stuffing them with herbs, onions, and sour pork. When I moved back to the Catskills, I still craved that dish, but the closest option was a solid two hour drive. I have a bit of an aversion to deep-frying at home unless it's absolutely necessary (the Baja-Style Fish Tacos on page 171 are an exception), so I wanted to try to make an at-home version for when ordering the real thing wasn't an option. This draws inspiration from the same flavors, without deep-frying.

This recipe works best with day-old rice, or preferably up to four-day-old, rice. The more time the rice is in the fridge, the dryer it becomes—and the crispier it becomes in the pan. If you don't have a few days to spare, make a batch of rice and spread it onto a parchment paper–lined baking sheet and place it in the fridge uncovered for an hour or two, then proceed with the recipe as instructed.

INGREDIENTS

Nuoc Cham
2 tablespoons fish sauce
2 tablespoons warm water
Zest of 2 limes
Juice of 3 limes
2 teaspoons light brown sugar
1 garlic clove, grated
1 teaspoon crushed red
  pepper flakes

Crispy Rice
6 tablespoons grapeseed oil
6 cups cooked white rice,
  preferably day-old
1 small red onion, thinly sliced
5 scallions (about 1 bunch),
  white and light green parts
  thinly sliced
½ cup mint leaves, roughly
  chopped
½ cup cilantro, leaves and
  stems finely chopped
½ cup basil leaves, roughly
  torn

DIRECTIONS

Make the nuoc cham: In a small bowl or glass measuring cup, add the fish sauce, water, lime zest and juice, brown sugar, garlic, and red pepper flakes, and whisk to combine.

Make the crispy rice: In a large pan or Dutch oven, heat 2 tablespoons of grapeseed oil over medium-high heat. Once the oil begins to shimmer, add 2 cups of rice and spread into an even layer with a spatula. Cook without stirring until the rice is lightly golden brown, about 5 minutes. The rice won't all hold together, so work your way around the pan, then flip and continue cooking until the rice is golden brown on the other side, about 5 minutes, then transfer to a large bowl.

Repeat with the remaining rice, 2 cups each time, and adding 2 tablespoons of grapeseed oil before frying each batch.

Add the onion, scallions, mint, cilantro, and basil to the bowl with the rice and drizzle the nuoc cham over it, stirring until combined. The crispy rice salad can be stored in a sealed container in the refrigerator for up to 3 days. The herbs may become slightly discolored but they're still fine to eat.

Use cilantro for the California Citrus Salad (page 55), Carrot Ribbon Salad (page 59), Charred Cauliflower with Zhoug and Pine Nuts (page 93), and Baja-Style Fish Tacos (page 171). Keep basil for the Chilled Green Soup (page 97), Orecchiette with Carrot Top Pesto and Peas (page 113), or Curried Mussels with Basil (page 166). Mint is wonderful in the Israeli Couscous with Herbs (page 125).

Farro with Mushrooms

Serves 2 to 4

This is one of my favorite ways to eat mushrooms. With soy sauce and a healthy handful of Parmesan—two ingredients that deliver major umami—the mushrooms take on an intensely savory and delicious flavor. It's exciting enough to be served as a dish all on its own—like risotto—or you can serve it as a side dish with Butter-Basted Lamb Chops (page 155) or Spatchcock Paprika Chicken with Carrots and Onions (page 129). I love the nutty, chewy flavor of farro, but you could easily swap in another type of grain like rice, barley, millet, or quinoa.

INGREDIENTS

1 cup farro
2 tablespoons olive oil
1 large shallot, finely chopped
2-inch knob ginger, minced
1 pound mixed mushrooms, such as shiitake, cremini, oyster, and trumpet, roughly chopped
3 garlic cloves, minced
2 tablespoons soy sauce
½ cup dry white wine, such as sauvignon blanc or pinot grigio
3 cups chicken or vegetable stock
1 cup grated Parmesan
¼ cup parsley leaves, roughly chopped

DIRECTIONS

Place the farro in a large fine-mesh sieve and run under cold water until the water runs clear.

Add the olive oil to a Dutch oven over medium-high heat. Once the oil begins to shimmer, add the shallot and ginger and cook, stirring often, until golden brown, about 2 minutes.

Add the mushrooms and cook, stirring occasionally, until they release some of their water and slightly wilt, about 3 minutes.

Add the garlic and soy sauce, and cook until the soy sauce evaporates and the mushrooms are fragrant, about 2 minutes.

Add the farro and stir to combine. Cook, stirring occasionally, until toasted and golden brown, about 2 minutes.

Add the wine and cook, scraping up any brown bits on the bottom of the pot, until the alcohol is burned off, about 2 minutes.

Add the stock, stir to combine, and bring to a boil. Place the lid on and reduce the heat to medium-low. Cook until the farro is tender and most of the stock is evaporated, about 55 minutes. Add the Parmesan and parsley and stir to combine. If not serving immediately, let cool to room temperature and store in a sealed container in the refrigerator for up to 3 days.

Save parsley for the Spicy Brothy Bacony Beans (page 115), Crispy Chicken Thighs with Chickpeas and Olives (page 133), Red Wine Braised Short Rib Ragout (page 137) or the Tuna and White Bean Salad (page 175). Store your Parmesan rind in the refrigerator for Spicy Brothy Bacony Beans (page 115) or Parmesan Broth (page 237). Use up ginger with the Olive Oil–Fried Egg with Chili Crisp (page 219), Whole Red Snapper with Cilantro and Lime (page 169), Curried Mussels with Basil (page 166), or Stone Fruit Crisp (page 179).

Israeli Couscous with Herbs

Serves 4

Israeli couscous is technically a pasta, but it looks like a grain and makes a great base for grain salads, so I've included it here. You can toss Israeli couscous with just about anything and it'll be good, but I like this combination of crunchy toasted walnuts, punchy preserved lemon, and a handful of herbs, a trio inspired by the flavors of the Middle East. This dish pairs equally well with meat or fish.

If you don't have preserved lemon on hand, use the zest of one lemon in its place.

INGREDIENTS

¾ cup raw walnuts
2 tablespoons olive oil, divided
1 cup Israeli couscous
1½ cups chicken or vegetable stock
1 teaspoon kosher salt, divided
1 preserved lemon, flesh removed, rind finely chopped
Juice of ½ lemon
1 cup mint leaves, roughly chopped
½ cup finely chopped dill
Flaky sea salt, to serve

DIRECTIONS

Add the walnuts to a small pan over medium heat and cook, stirring often, until lightly toasted, about 2 minutes. Transfer the walnuts to a cutting board to cool to room temperature, then roughly chop.

Add 1 tablespoon of olive oil to a medium pot over medium-high heat. Once the oil begins to shimmer, add the couscous and cook, stirring occasionally, until toasted, about 2 minutes.

Add the stock and ½ teaspoon of salt and bring to a boil. Place the lid on and reduce the heat to low and simmer for 10 minutes. Drain the couscous through a fine-mesh sieve.

In a large bowl, add the remaining 1 tablespoon of olive oil, the remaining ½ teaspoon of salt, the preserved lemon, walnuts, and couscous and stir to combine. Add the lemon juice, mint, and dill and stir to combine. Serve with a pinch of flaky sea salt. The couscous lasts for up to 3 days in a sealed container in the refrigerator. In order to keep the herbs from browning, add them just before serving.

Try making your own Preserved Lemons (page 227). You can use preserved lemons in the Creamy Preserved Lemon Pasta (page 109). If you have leftover mint, add it to the Crispy Rice Salad (page 121). Use up dill in the Halibut with Tomatoes and Dill (page 161) or the Crispy Sweet Potato Skins with Crème Fraîche (page 47). Extra walnuts can be saved for the Celery Salad with Walnuts and Pecorino (page 63), Hanger Steak with Walnut Romesco (page 143), White Wine Braised Leeks (page 75), or the One-Bowl Fudgy Brownies (page 195).

MEAT

Spatchcock Paprika Chicken with Carrots and Onions

Crispy Chicken Thighs with Chickpeas and Olives

Herby Chicken Salad

Really Good Meatballs

Red Wine Braised Short Rib Ragout

Smash Burger

Hanger Steak with Walnut Romesco

Sausage and DIY Kraut

Mustardy Pork Tenderloin with Grapes and Red Onion

Pork Shoulder Larb

Butter-Basted Lamb Chops

Lamb Phyllo Pie

Spatchcock Paprika Chicken with Carrots and Onions

Serves 4

Spatchcocking a bird can seem intimidating, but the process is easier than you think. Use a pair of kitchen shears (although I've used garden shears in a pinch) to cut out the chicken's backbone, then flatten the chicken by pressing down with your hands. This yields a chicken—or turkey!—that cooks faster. Spatchcocking also makes it faster to divvy up the chicken when it's done cooking. Since it's already flattened, there's no maneuvering around the chicken trying to carve the perfect pieces. Just slice at the joints, plate, and eat.

I rub this spatchcock chicken with a heaping spoonful of paprika for some color and warmth, and a dash of cayenne for some heat. It cooks over carrots, onions, lemons, and capers, which soften as they baste in the chicken's juices. Make sure to spoon any leftover juices in the bottom of the pan over the chicken and vegetables when you serve this—it makes a delicious pan sauce. Or better yet, sop it up with a hunk of bread.

To ensure the carrots and onions are cooked properly, I start roasting them before the bird. If you don't have enough carrots on hand, swap in parsnips, turnips, or parsley root, or another type of root vegetable. And save the backbone and carcass from the chicken to make your own stock. I throw mine into a bag and store it in the freezer until I've gathered enough vegetable scraps to make chicken stock.

INGREDIENTS

4 tablespoons olive oil, divided

3 teaspoons kosher salt, divided

2 teaspoons freshly ground black pepper

1 tablespoon paprika

¼ teaspoon cayenne pepper

1 bunch medium carrots, halved lengthwise

2 medium yellow onions, cut into eighths

1 lemon, quartered

2 tablespoons capers, drained and rinsed

1 whole chicken (about 4 pounds)

DIRECTIONS

Preheat the oven to 400°F. Add 2 tablespoons of olive oil, 2 teaspoons of salt, the black pepper, paprika, and cayenne to a small bowl and whisk to combine.

Arrange the carrots, onions, and lemon wedges in the bottom of a large cast iron or stainless steel pan, or a large baking dish. Sprinkle the capers, the remaining 2 tablespoons of olive oil, and the remaining 1 teaspoon of salt over the vegetables and use your hands to gently toss until well coated. Roast until the vegetables are just fork-tender, about 20 minutes.

While the vegetables are roasting, prepare the chicken. If your chicken has giblets, remove them from the cavity and reserve for a later use, such as chicken stock. Pat the chicken dry all over with paper towels, including the cavity.

Place the chicken breast-side down on a cutting board. Using sharp kitchen shears, cut along one side of the backbone from the tail to the neck, all the way through the chicken. Then cut along the other side of the backbone. Save the backbone for stock. Flip the chicken so it's breast-side up and use your hand to press firmly on the breastbone to flatten the chicken until you hear a snap. Rub the chicken all over with the spice mixture.

Continued on next page

Carefully remove the pan from the oven and place the chicken on top of the vegetables, breast-side up.

Return the pan to the oven and roast the chicken until golden brown all over, 55 to 60 minutes, or until a meat thermometer inserted in the thickest part of the chicken reaches 165°F.

Let the chicken rest for at least 10 minutes before carving. Serve with the pan juices spooned over the chicken. The cooked chicken can be stored in a sealed container in the refrigerator for up to 3 days.

Save the chicken carcass for Chicken Stock (page 234). Any leftover chicken can be shredded and used for the Herby Chicken Salad (page 134).

Crispy Chicken Thighs with Chickpeas and Olives

Serves 4

We all have different weeknight dinner routines, but I think this recipe fits most: it comes together in one pot, in less than one hour. Chicken thighs are seared until golden brown. Spiced chickpeas are toasted, doused in white wine and melted chicken fat, then spooned over those crispy chicken thighs. This is a rich and hearty dish, so I've added a handful of Castelvetrano olives—you can use any green olives in your pantry—and lemon juice, which both add some brightness.

INGREDIENTS

6 bone-in, skin-on chicken thighs
1½ teaspoons kosher salt, divided
Freshly ground black pepper
2 teaspoons dried oregano
1 tablespoon olive oil
5 medium shallots, quartered
1 head garlic, cloves peeled and lightly smashed
2 cans (15.5 ounces each) chickpeas, drained and rinsed
½ teaspoon crushed red pepper flakes
1 teaspoon ground cumin
½ cup dry white wine, such as sauvignon blanc or pinot grigio
¾ cup pitted Castelvetrano olives, smashed
¾ cup low-sodium chicken stock
1 cup (½ bunch) roughly chopped parsley leaves and tender stems
Juice of 1 lemon

DIRECTIONS

Preheat the oven to 375°F.

On a cutting board, pat the chicken thighs dry with a paper towel. Season both sides with ½ teaspoon of salt, the black pepper, and oregano.

Heat the olive oil in a large pan or Dutch oven that's big enough to fit all the chicken thighs in one layer over medium-high heat. Once the oil begins to shimmer, add the chicken thighs skin-side down and cook without moving until the skin is golden brown, 6 to 8 minutes. Flip the chicken thighs and continue cooking until golden brown on the other side, 2 to 3 minutes. Transfer the chicken thighs to a paper towel–lined plate.

Reduce the heat to medium. Add the shallots and garlic to the pan and cook until golden brown, 2 to 3 minutes. Add the chickpeas, the remaining 1 teaspoon of salt, the red pepper flakes, and cumin and stir to combine. Cook until the chickpeas begin to turn golden brown, about 5 minutes.

Increase the heat to high and add the wine, scraping up any brown bits on the bottom of the pan. Cook until the smell of alcohol burns off and the wine is simmering, about 2 minutes. Add the olives and stock and return to a simmer.

Place the chicken skin-side up on top of the chickpeas, then transfer to the oven uncovered. Bake until cooked through or the internal temperature reaches 165°F, 25 to 30 minutes.

Transfer the chicken thighs to a plate. Place the pan back on the stove over medium-high heat and reduce the chickpea mixture until the liquid is nearly all evaporated, about 10 minutes. Add the parsley and lemon juice and stir to combine. Serve the chicken thighs topped with a scoop of chickpeas. The chicken can be stored in a sealed container in the refrigerator for up to 3 days.

Save those chicken bones for Chicken Stock (page 234). If you have extra chicken, use it for the Herby Chicken Salad (page 134). Extra Castelvetrano olives can be used for the Bucatini with Tuna and Olives (page 107) or Mixed Olive Tapenade (page 44).

Herby Chicken Salad

Serves 4

Chicken salad is the easiest way to use up leftover chicken. The thing is, I've never really liked it. The idea of cubed chicken makes me shudder. (I don't have a reason, it just does.) So I set out to make a version I could actually get excited about, and it starts with shredding the chicken into big, juicy hunks. This is the time to make use of rotisserie chicken, or any leftovers you might have—perhaps from the Spatchcock Paprika Chicken with Carrots and Onions (page 129).

I've also added lots of herbs and a secret ingredient: Kewpie mayonnaise. Kewpie is a brand of Japanese mayonnaise made with egg yolks and rice vinegar, which makes for a richer, creamier mayo spread with just a hint of sweetness. If you don't have it readily available, you can make something similar with pantry ingredients. Add 2 tablespoons of mayonnaise with ¾ teaspoon of rice vinegar and ⅛ teaspoon of sugar and mix to combine.

INGREDIENTS

2 tablespoons Kewpie mayonnaise
1 tablespoon olive oil
Zest of 1 lemon
2 tablespoons lemon juice
2 scallions, white and light green parts thinly sliced
2 tablespoons finely chopped basil
2 tablespoons finely chopped parsley leaves and stems
2 tablespoons finely chopped cilantro leaves and stems
½ teaspoon kosher salt
¼ teaspoon freshly ground black pepper
3 cups shredded chicken

DIRECTIONS

In a large bowl, add the mayonnaise, olive oil, lemon zest and juice, scallions, basil, parsley, cilantro, salt, and pepper, and mix until smooth. Add the chicken and stir until well combined. The chicken salad can be stored in a sealed container and kept in the refrigerator for up to 3 days.

Use up Kewpie mayonnaise in the BLT Salad (page 57). Keep cilantro for the California Citrus Salad (page 55), Carrot Ribbon Salad (page 59), Charred Cauliflower with Zhoug and Pine Nuts (page 93), or Baja-Style Fish Tacos (page 171). Save parsley for the Spicy Brothy Bacony Beans (page 115), Farro with Mushrooms (page 123), Crispy Chicken Thighs with Chickpeas and Olives (page 133), Red Wine Braised Short Rib Ragout (page 137), or the Tuna and White Bean Salad (page 175). Use basil for the Chilled Green Soup (page 97), Orechiette with Carrot Top Pesto and Peas (page 113), or Curried Mussels with Basil (page 166).

Really Good Meatballs

Makes about 24 meatballs

A few years ago, I wrote a piece for one of my favorite recipe sites, The Kitchn, comparing meatball recipes to find out which one was the best. After a week of making nothing but meatballs, I discovered that the best ones all followed the same philosophy: more is more.

This recipe amps up the flavor in every way. Shallots get cooked in bacon fat along with garlic and red pepper flakes, which is so good, frankly you could just eat it slathered on crusty bread. But then shallots get mixed with beef and pork, cornmeal, and plenty of Parm, for what I believe are the best of the best meatballs.

Oh, and they happen to be gluten-free! And they keep your kitchen clean, as I recommend you bake these—the meatball stays moist this way—rather than frying them.

INGREDIENTS

6 strips bacon, thinly sliced (about 1 cup)
1 large shallot, minced
2 garlic cloves, minced
1 teaspoon crushed red pepper flakes
1 cup cornmeal
¼ cup water
1 pound 85% lean/15% fat ground beef
1 pound 80% lean/20% fat ground pork
1 cup grated Parmesan
2 large eggs, lightly beaten
1 tablespoon Worcestershire sauce
2 teaspoons kosher salt
1 teaspoon freshly ground black pepper
¾ cup finely chopped parsley

DIRECTIONS

Preheat the oven to 400°F. Line a rimmed baking sheet with foil.

Heat a large pan over medium-high heat. Once the pan is hot, add the bacon and cook, stirring occasionally, until the bacon begins to crisp, 6 to 8 minutes. Add the shallot and cook until it begins to soften and the bacon is really crispy, about 2 minutes. Add the garlic and red pepper flakes and cook for about 1 minute, or until aromatic. Transfer the bacon and shallot mixture to a paper towel–lined plate with a slotted spoon. Let cool for 5 minutes.

In a small bowl, stir the cornmeal and water until combined.

In a large bowl, add the ground beef, ground pork, Parmesan, eggs, Worcestershire sauce, salt, black pepper, parsley, cornmeal, and bacon mixture, and use your hands to mix until well combined, without overworking it too much.

Roll the meat into 1½-inch balls and place on the prepared baking sheet. Alternatively, the meatballs can be frozen. To freeze, place the meatballs on the baking sheet and transfer to the freezer until frozen. Once frozen, the meatballs can be placed in a sealed container and stored for up to 3 months.

Bake the meatballs until just cooked through and the internal temperature reaches 160°F, about 16 minutes, or 20 to 25 minutes if previously frozen. The meatballs can be stored in a sealed container in the refrigerator for up to 3 days. Serve with pasta and the sauce from the Eggplant Parmesan (page 85).

Save that Parmesan rind for Parmesan Broth (page 237), Spicy Brothy Bacony Beans (page 115), Chicken Stock (page 234), or Corn Stock (page 235). Cornmeal can be used in place of polenta for the Creamy Gruyère Polenta (page 119). Extra bacon can be used for the BLT Salad (page 57).

Red Wine Braised Short Rib Ragout

Serves 6

There's pretty much nothing I want more than a big pot of braised short ribs when the first snow hits the ground. I like serving these with the Creamy Gruyère Polenta (page 119), but you could also pair it with egg noodles or a few slices of crusty bread. You've spent some time making this decadent sauce—enjoy every last bite.

Short ribs are really all about leaning into comfort, so I use a whole bottle of wine here. I've found it adds the right amount of body (and acidity) to the sauce, and you don't have to worry about half a bottle going bad in the fridge. Win-win. If you're abstaining from wine, use three cups of stock in its place.

INGREDIENTS

4 pounds English-style bone-in short ribs

Kosher salt

Freshly ground black pepper

2 tablespoons olive oil

1 large yellow onion, finely chopped

3 medium carrots, finely chopped

2 leeks, white and light green parts only, thinly sliced

4 garlic cloves, thinly sliced

½ bunch parsley, stems finely chopped, leaves roughly chopped, divided

3 anchovies or

1½ teaspoons anchovy paste

1 bottle dry red wine

2 cups beef or chicken stock

2 tablespoons balsamic vinegar

DIRECTIONS

Preheat the oven to 300°F.

On a cutting board, generously season the short ribs with salt and pepper on all sides.

In a Dutch oven or large oven-safe pot, heat the olive oil over high heat. Once the oil begins to shimmer, add the short ribs and sear on all sides until golden brown, about 3 minutes per side. You may need to work in batches depending on the size of the pot. Transfer the short ribs to a paper towel–lined plate.

Drain all but 2 tablespoons of fat from the pot—you just need enough to coat the bottom of the pot in a thin layer. Over medium-high heat, add the onion, carrots, and leeks, and cook until golden brown and softened, about 8 minutes.

Add the garlic, parsley stems, and anchovies, and stir to combine, using a wooden spoon to break up the anchovies. Cook until the garlic is softened and the anchovies have dissolved, about 3 minutes.

Add the wine and scrape up any brown bits from the bottom of the pot. Bring to a boil, cooking until the smell of alcohol burns off, about 3 minutes.

Add the short ribs and stock and bring to a boil.

Place the lid on the pot and transfer to the oven. Braise until the meat easily pulls away from the bones, about 3½ hours.

Remove the meat from the pot and transfer to a bowl. Discard the bones and use two forks to shred the meat.

Continued on next page

Skim about half of the fat from the surface of the braising liquid and discard. Set the pot over medium-high heat and bring the liquid back to a boil. Reduce the heat to medium-low and simmer for 30 to 45 minutes, until reduced by three-fourths. The sauce should be thick and glossy.

Add the meat back to the pot with the sauce. Add the vinegar and cook for 5 minutes over medium heat.

Add half of the chopped parsley leaves and stir to combine. Top the ragout with the remaining parsley and serve with pasta, polenta, or bread. The ragout can be stored in a sealed container in the refrigerator for up to 3 days, or frozen for up to 3 months.

Use up the open can of anchovies in the Green Goddess Salad (page 53), Mixed Olive Tapenade (page 44), or the Shaved Zucchini with Bagna Cauda (page 61). Save the leek tops for the Fingerling Potato and Leek Top Frittata (page 215). Use carrots in the Lentil Soup with Parsley (page 117), Chicken Stock (page 234), Spatchcock Paprika Chicken with Carrots and Onions (page 129), or Carrot Ribbon Salad (page 59). Use the rest of the parsley for Squash with Herby Salsa Verde (page 101), Greens Skillet Pie (page 83), Bucatini with Tuna and Olives (page 107), Roasted Radishes and Turnips with Brown Butter Caper Sauce (page 91), Spicy Brothy Bacony Beans (page 115), Crispy Chicken Thighs with Chickpeas and Olives (page 133), or Herby Chicken Salad (page 134).

Smash Burger

Serves 2 to 4

I've always loved burgers. When I was growing up, whenever we'd visit my dad's family in Ohio, we'd stop at Skyway, a drive-in restaurant where the waiters zip up to the cars on roller skates. It's still one of my favorite places to eat. We always ordered the burger—a thin patty, smashed so the edges got crispy, topped with mustard, pickles, and onions with a tall grape soda on the side. Since then, I've cooked and eaten a lot of burgers, but the Skyway version remains my idea of what a good burger should be. I've taken inspiration from it, but I've added a layer of cheddar cheese, a smear of Thousand Island dressing, and a handful of pickles. You might notice it's the same recipe as the Poached Shrimp with Thousand Island dressing (page 25). Can you tell I'm a fan?

When I say smash, I mean it: wrap a heavy object, like a brick or a cast iron pan, in foil and use it in place of a spatula to flatten that ground beef. The thinner the burger, the crispier the edges will get. Spatulas never get the burgers quite thin enough, in my opinion.

INGREDIENTS

Thousand Island Dressing

¾ cup mayonnaise

¼ cup ketchup

2 tablespoons finely chopped pickles

1 garlic clove, minced

2 teaspoons champagne vinegar

Burgers

12 ounces 80% lean/ 20% fat ground beef

1 to 2 teaspoons kosher salt

1 teaspoon freshly ground black pepper

1 teaspoon grapeseed oil

4 slices cheddar cheese

4 Hawaiian sweet hamburger buns

Pickles, to serve

DIRECTIONS

Make the Thousand Island dressing: In a medium bowl, whisk the mayonnaise, ketchup, pickles, garlic, and vinegar. Store in a sealed container in the refrigerator until ready to serve. The Thousand Island dressing can be made up to 3 days in advance.

Make the burgers: Cover a heavy medium pan, brick, or cast iron pan with foil so the bottom is completely covered.

On a cutting board, divide the ground beef into four 3-ounce portions and roll into balls. Generously season the top of each ball with salt and pepper.

Heat the grapeseed oil in a cast iron or stainless steel pan over high heat until nearly smoking. Place two of the beef balls, seasoned-side down, in the pan and press down with your foil-covered object, forming a thin patty. Season with more salt and pepper. Cook until browned, 1 to 2 minutes.

Use a spatula to flip the burger. Place a slice of cheddar on each burger and cook until the burgers are cooked through and the cheese is melted, about 1 minute more. Repeat with the remaining two beef balls.

Place the burgers on the hamburger buns and top with Thousand Island dressing and pickles. Serve immediately. We rarely have leftover burgers in my house, but they'll stay good in a sealed container in the refrigerator for up to 3 days.

Serve leftover dressing for Poached Shrimp with Thousand Island Dressing (page 25).

Sausage and DIY Kraut

Serves 4

This recipe is really all about sauerkraut. I love all things fermented, and so does my friend Riss. When I asked about her fermenting techniques, Riss recommended I check out Sandor Katz, a fermentation guru. He's known for his sauerkraut—so much so that he earned the charming nickname Sandorkraut. This recipe was inspired by his technique, which he says is based on tradition and intuition.

As for the sausage, you can use any type here, but bratwurst and kraut are a classic combo. There are so many ways to cook sausage—grilled, boiled, broiled—but I found the combination of simmering and searing to lead to the most consistent results: snappy on the outside, perfectly cooked through on the inside. Celery seeds are optional, since I don't want you to skip making kraut if you don't have them on hand, but I think they add a floral flavor to the cabbage, making this kraut taste lighter and brighter. On that note, cabbage is a great place to start if you're making sauerkraut for the first time, but you can add other hardy vegetables like carrots, turnips, radishes, and beets using this same method.

INGREDIENTS

Sauerkraut
½ large green cabbage
1 tablespoon kosher salt
½ teaspoon celery seeds, optional

Sausage
1 pound bratwurst
½ teaspoon grapeseed oil

Whole grain mustard, to serve

DIRECTIONS

Make the sauerkraut: It's imperative that you clean your work surface and all your tools before getting started to ensure no bad bacteria grows in the kraut. Use ample soap and water, and dry carefully. Set a mandoline over a large bowl. Carefully use the mandoline to slice the cabbage into 1⁄16-inch slices, including the core. Alternatively, you can thinly slice the cabbage on a cutting board with a chef's knife.

Add the salt to the cabbage and use your fists to press down on the cabbage, rocking them back and forth to shrink the cabbage, for at least 5 minutes. The salt will draw liquid from the cabbage. You're ready to move to the next step when there are at least 2 tablespoons of liquid in the bottom of the bowl. If you're using celery seeds, add them now, mixing until evenly combined.

Transfer the cabbage and liquid to a large jar or 32-ounce deli container and press it down so the cabbage is submerged in the liquid. Fill a smaller vessel, such as a ramekin, or another 32-ounce deli container, with water and place it on top of the cabbage to weight it down.

Place the cabbage in a cool, dark space for at least 1 week until it has shrunken further and begun to ferment. Taste the kraut to see how sour it is. If you want a more intense flavor, continue to ferment, making sure to check daily, until it reaches your desired flavor. Once it does, store the kraut in a sealed container in the refrigerator for up to 2 months.

Continued on next page

Make the sausage: Place the sausage in a medium pan and cover with cold water. Set over medium-high heat, bring to a simmer, and cook for 10 minutes. Transfer the sausages to a paper towel–lined plate and dry completely.

Heat the grapeseed oil in a medium pan over medium heat. Once the oil begins to shimmer, add the sausage and cook, without moving, until browned on one side, about 4 minutes. Repeat with the remaining sides, until browned all over.

Serve the sausage with a heaping side of kraut and some whole grain mustard. Sausage can be stored in a sealed container in the refrigerator for up to 3 days.

Use the other half of the green cabbage alongside the Pork Shoulder Larb (page 151) or thinly sliced for the Baja-Style Fish Tacos (page 171).

Mustardy Pork Tenderloin with Grapes and Red Onions

Serves 2 to 4

This pork tenderloin is surprisingly simple, and one of my go-to recipes. What makes this an all-time great for me is the grapes. Trust me on the grapes—as they roast, they soften and become almost saucy. This is the perfect way to use up any that have started to lose their firmness, as they'll cook down so much it'll be unnoticeable. They cook alongside red onions and the mustard-slathered pork, which means this dish walks the line between sweet, spicy, and savory. This recipe can be easily doubled and makes great leftovers reheated or straight from the fridge.

Tenderloin is not to be confused with pork loin, a wider, flatter cut that comes from an entirely different part of the pig. While I'm all about swaps, these two cuts can't be used interchangeably without adjusting the cooking time, so make sure you buy the right type of loin.

INGREDIENTS

1½ pounds pork tenderloin
1 teaspoon kosher salt
½ teaspoon freshly ground black pepper
1½ tablespoons Dijon mustard
2 tablespoons grapeseed oil
2 cups (½ bunch) seedless red grapes
1 red onion, thinly sliced
½ teaspoon crushed red pepper flakes

DIRECTIONS

Preheat the oven to 425°F.

On a cutting board, pat the pork tenderloin dry with paper towels. Season with the salt and black pepper on all sides, then rub the tenderloin with the Dijon.

Heat the grapeseed oil in a cast iron or stainless steel pan over medium-high heat. Once the oil begins to shimmer, add the tenderloin and sear on all sides until browned, about 4 minutes per side. Add the grapes, onion, and red pepper flakes, then transfer to the oven. Roast for 15 to 18 minutes, or until the internal temperature of the tenderloin reaches 135°F.

Remove the tenderloin from the pan and transfer to a cutting board to rest for 10 minutes before slicing. Meanwhile, place the pan back in the oven to continue roasting until the grapes have cooked down and collapsed on themselves, 8 to 10 minutes.

Slice the pork and serve topped with the onion and grapes. The pork can be stored in a sealed container in the refrigerator for up to 3 days.

Make a Fruit Shrub (page 241) with leftover grapes or save them for the Any Fruit Granita (page 205). They're also a good addition to This is How You Make a Cheese Plate (page 27).

Pork Shoulder Larb

Serves 8 to 10

One of my favorite Thai restaurants in Los Angeles, Hoy-ka, consistently has a line out the door. Everything on the menu is fantastic, but my all-time favorite dishes are the larb. Every time I go I order the off-menu crispy pork larb. Larb is originally a Laotian dish, although it's also eaten in the Isan region of Thailand. Crispy pork belly is mixed with chilies, thinly sliced red onions, and lots of herbs. Toasted and ground rice adds a subtle crunch and helps bind the dish together. Early in 2020, when restaurants were still closed due to the pandemic, I constantly craved that dish from Hoy-Ka. Inspired by what they do so well, I went to the grocery store, but couldn't find pork belly anywhere. I picked up a pork shoulder instead. It's not traditional, but it delivered a succulent, melt-in-your-mouth pork flavor I craved. With many thanks to Hoy-ka for all they do, and for their inspiration here, I present an interpretation of that dish.

Make sure to save the braising liquid here for simmering a pot of beans, rice, or farro later. It keeps for up to three days in a sealed container in the fridge, and freezes well for up to three months. To prepare the lemongrass, remove the tough outer leaves and the tough bulb. Thinly slice the white and very pale green parts, which should be about two to three inches of the stalk itself. If you can't find lemongrass, use the zest of one lemon per one stalk for a similar flavor.

INGREDIENTS

4 pounds boneless pork shoulder

3½ tablespoons kosher salt, divided

¼ cup light brown sugar, divided

1 tablespoon freshly ground black pepper

2 teaspoons ground coriander

2 tablespoons grapeseed oil

4 cups chicken stock

½ cup white rice

½ red onion, thinly sliced lengthwise

Zest and juice of 6 limes

¼ cup fish sauce

2 teaspoons crushed red pepper flakes

2 tablespoons lemongrass (from 1 stalk), thinly sliced

1 bunch cilantro, roughly chopped

DIRECTIONS

Preheat the oven to 300°F.

Pat the pork shoulder dry with paper towels.

In a bowl, whisk 3 tablespoons of salt, 2 tablespoons of brown sugar, the black pepper, and coriander. Rub the spice mixture all over the pork shoulder in an even layer.

Heat the grapeseed oil in a Dutch oven or large oven-safe pot over medium-high heat. Once the oil begins to shimmer, add the pork shoulder and sear on all sides until golden brown, about 3 minutes per side.

Add the stock and bring to a simmer. Place the lid on the pot and transfer to the oven. Braise the pork shoulder until the pork is very tender and easily shreds with a fork, about 4 hours.

Remove the pork and transfer to a cutting board to rest to room temperature. Reserve the braising liquid for another use in a sealed container in the refrigerator. Pull the meat apart into bite-size pieces with two forks.

While the pork is cooling, heat a medium pan over medium heat. Add the rice and toast, stirring often, until golden brown, about 5 minutes.

Continued on next page

1 bunch mint, roughly
  chopped
1 small green cabbage,
  quartered, to serve
1 English cucumber, sliced
  into thick coins, to serve
1 lime, cut into wedges, to
  serve

Transfer the toasted rice to a spice grinder, mini food processor, or mortar and pestle and process or pound until finely ground.

In a large bowl, add the onion, lime zest and juice, fish sauce, the remaining 2 tablespoons of brown sugar, the red pepper flakes, lemongrass, cilantro, and mint, and stir to combine. Let the mixture sit at room temperature for 10 minutes to let the onions soften.

Add the pork, ground rice, and the remaining 1½ teaspoons of salt and stir to combine. Serve the larb with the cabbage, cucumbers, and lime wedges. The pork shoulder larb can be stored in a sealed container in the refrigerator for up to 3 days.

Rice is a staple in my pantry, but if you're looking to use up some of the ingredients, make a Crispy Rice Salad (page 121)—it also uses fish sauce and a lot of the same herbs. Use the other half of the red onion for the Crispy Sweet Potato Skins with Crème Fraîche (page 47), or the California Citrus Salad (page 55). Extra lemongrass can be saved for the Lemongrass Syrup (page 242).

Butter-Basted Lamb Chops

Serves 2 to 4

It doesn't take much to make lamb chops into a great dinner. A handful of hardy herbs, garlic, a spoonful of mustard, and a knob of butter go a long way.

Unlike with a larger roast, I only marinate chops for an hour or two. Any longer and you run the risk of the acid in the marinade breaking down the proteins in the meat, resulting in a gray, mushy chop. If you're short on time, fifteen minutes will do—you just want to capture the flavor of the aromatics before searing. I prefer my lamb on the rare side, but if too much pink scares you, cook them for three minutes per side.

INGREDIENTS
¼ cup finely chopped sage leaves

¼ cup finely chopped thyme leaves

4 garlic cloves, minced

1 tablespoon Dijon mustard

4 tablespoons olive oil, divided

2 teaspoons kosher salt

1 teaspoon freshly ground black pepper

1½ pounds lamb chops

1 tablespoon unsalted butter

DIRECTIONS
In a large bowl, stir the sage, thyme, garlic, Dijon, 3 tablespoons of olive oil, the salt, and pepper. Add the lamb chops and use your hands to evenly coat them with the herb mixture. Cover the bowl with plastic wrap and refrigerate for at least 1 hour, or up to 2 hours.

Remove the lamb chops from the refrigerator 15 minutes before cooking.

Heat the remaining 1 tablespoon of olive oil in a large pan over high heat. Once the oil begins to shimmer, add half of the lamb chops, making sure not to crowd the pan (add less if necessary). Cook, without moving, until golden brown on one side, 2½ to 3 minutes, depending on how rare you like your meat. Flip the chops with tongs and add ½ tablespoon of butter to the pan, and continue cooking until golden brown on the other side, another 2½ to 3 minutes. As the butter melts, spoon it over the lamb chops. Repeat with the remaining chops and butter.

The lamb chops can be served hot or at room temperature. They can be stored in a sealed container in the refrigerator for up to 3 days.

Leftover sage can be used for Fried Sage Leaves (page 41). Use up that bunch of thyme for the Root Vegetable Pot Pie (page 88), Marinated Ricotta Salata with Cracked Spices (page 33), or White Wine Braised Leeks (page 75).

Lamb Phyllo Pie

Serves 4 to 6

This recipe combines two of my favorite things: phyllo and pie. There's not much I find more satisfying than cutting through thin, crackly layers of phyllo. And I'll find any excuse to eat anything pielike, especially if it's savory. Here, phyllo envelops spiced lamb studded with feta, chilies, and cilantro stems. I like to serve this with a big pile of fresh herbs on top, which helps cut the richness of the lamb and adds a bright, herbaceous bite.

INGREDIENTS

- 3 tablespoons olive oil, divided, plus more for greasing
- 1 medium yellow onion, halved and thinly sliced
- 3 large garlic cloves, minced
- 3 small dried red chilies, stems removed, sliced into ¼-inch pieces, or ½ teaspoon crushed red pepper flakes
- 2 teaspoons kosher salt
- 2 teaspoons ground cumin
- 1 teaspoon ground coriander
- 1 teaspoon paprika
- ¼ teaspoon sugar
- 1 pound ground lamb
- 1 cup crumbled feta
- 8 ounces frozen phyllo dough (1 roll, half of a 16-ounce package), thawed
- 1 cup (½ bunch) cilantro, stems finely chopped, leaves roughly chopped, divided
- ½ bunch mint, roughly torn

DIRECTIONS

Preheat the oven to 350°F.

Heat 1 tablespoon of olive oil in a large skillet over medium-high heat. Once the oil begins to shimmer, add the onion and cook, stirring frequently, until softened and lightly golden, about 8 minutes.

Add the garlic and chilies and cook for about 1 minute, or until fragrant. Add the salt, cumin, coriander, paprika, and sugar, and stir to combine. Cook, stirring frequently, until fragrant, about 1 minute more.

Add the lamb and break up with a wooden spoon. Cook, stirring occasionally and scraping up any brown bits on the bottom of the skillet, until well browned and starting to crisp along the edges, about 8 minutes.

Remove the skillet from the heat. Add the feta and stir to combine.

Set a medium stainless steel or cast iron pan on the counter and brush it with olive oil. Take two sheets of phyllo dough and carefully alternate the direction of the layers so the pan is well covered. Continue with the remaining phyllo. Carefully press the phyllo to the center of the pan, creating a flat bottom, then spoon the lamb into the pan in an even layer. Using the remaining 2 tablespoons of olive oil, brush the exposed layers of phyllo, folding them in to create a circle around the lamb, leaving the center exposed.

Bake until the phyllo is golden brown and crispy, about 40 minutes. Carefully slide the pie out and place on a flat serving dish. Serve the pie topped with the cilantro leaves and mint. Lamb phyllo pie can be stored in a sealed container in the refrigerator for up to 3 days, but the phyllo will get soggy over time.

Use the other roll of phyllo dough in that package to make Baklava (page 199). Extra dried red chilies are a great addition to the Olive Oil–Fried Egg with Chili Crisp (page 219). Save cilantro for the Squash with Herby Salsa Verde (page 101), California Citrus Salad (page 55), Carrot Ribbon Salad (page 59), Charred Cauliflower with Zhoug and Pine Nuts (page 93), and Baja-Style Fish Tacos (page 171). Mint is key in the Israeli Couscous with Herbs (page 125).

SEAFOOD

Halibut with Tomatoes and Dill

Black Garlic Butter Salmon with Scallions

Clams with Chorizo and Fennel

Curried Mussels with Basil

Whole Red Snapper with Cilantro and Lime

Baja-Style Fish Tacos

Ceviche Tostada

Tuna and White Bean Salad

Halibut with Tomatoes and Dill

Serves 4

I know halibut is on the pricey side, and it's a high-stakes game when making it for the first time. But I swear this method is foolproof. The halibut gets baked in lots of olive oil infused with lemon, dill, shallots, and tomatoes, which helps keep the fish from drying out. There's a five-minute time range for when this fish will be done, so start checking at twenty minutes and keep an eye on it from there by gently nudging the fillet with a fork. If the flesh easily flakes and is opaque, it's ready.

INGREDIENTS

1 teaspoon black peppercorns
1 lemon, thinly sliced, seeds removed
1½-pounds center-cut, skin-off halibut fillet
3 cups (2 pints) cherry tomatoes, halved
1 medium shallot, thinly sliced lengthwise
4 garlic cloves, thinly sliced
5 sprigs dill, fronds only
1½ teaspoons kosher salt
¾ cup olive oil

DIRECTIONS

Preheat the oven to 300°F.

In a mortar, add the peppercorns and crush with a pestle. Alternatively, you can use the back of a chef's knife to press down on the peppercorns until they crack.

Lay the lemon slices on the bottom of a 9×13-inch baking dish and place the halibut on top. Arrange the tomatoes, shallot, garlic, and dill around the halibut and season with the salt and cracked peppercorns. Pour the olive oil over the top, making sure the halibut is entirely coated with oil.

Transfer the baking dish to the oven and roast until the halibut is just cooked through and easily flakes when nudged with a fork, 20 to 25 minutes.

Serve the halibut with the tomato mixture spooned on top. The halibut can be stored in a sealed container in the refrigerator for up to 3 days.

Use up the rest of that dill for the Crispy Sweet Potato Skins with Crème Fraîche (page 47), Israeli Couscous with Herbs (page 125), or the Greens Skillet Pie (page 83).

Black Garlic Butter Salmon with Scallions

Serves 4

On my laziest days I lean into the fact that it doesn't take a lot of work to make a piece of salmon taste good. This recipe starts out with a simple compound butter (which just means butter infused with other ingredients) made up of sweet, funky black garlic (for flavor), brown sugar (which helps with caramelization), and crushed red pepper flakes (for a little heat), which comes together in minutes before being slathered over the salmon. I opt for broiling my salmon to ensure a lacquered, almost blackened exterior and perfectly cooked center.

The flavor of black garlic is so unique there's really no way to substitute it. It's one of the only ingredients I'll ask you to go out of your way for, and I promise it's worth seeking out. Order it online at Food52, Whole Foods, or check out a specialty grocery store near you.

INGREDIENTS

4 black garlic cloves
3 tablespoons unsalted butter, at room temperature
1 tablespoon light brown sugar
1 teaspoon crushed red pepper flakes
1¼ teaspoons kosher salt, divided
1 to 1¼ pounds center-cut salmon fillet
2 bunches scallions, end and top inch of greens trimmed and discarded
1½ tablespoons olive oil

DIRECTIONS

Preheat the oven to broil on high.

Use the side of a knife to smash the garlic into a paste. Add the garlic paste to a small bowl with the butter, brown sugar, red pepper flakes, and 1 teaspoon of salt, and stir until combined. Rub the garlic butter all over the top of the salmon fillet.

Add the scallions to a rimmed baking sheet and drizzle with the olive oil and sprinkle with the remaining ¼ teaspoon of salt. Use your hands to coat the scallions with the oil. Move the scallions to the edges of the baking sheet, leaving space in the center for the salmon.

Place the scallions under the broiler until bright green and just wilted, about 2 minutes.

Carefully remove the baking sheet from the oven and place the salmon fillet in the center, then broil until the scallions are lightly charred and the salmon is just cooked through and flakes easily with a fork, or until the internal temperature reaches 120°F, about 7 minutes. Serve the salmon topped with the scallions. The salmon can be stored in a sealed container in the refrigerator for up to 3 days.

Use extra black garlic in the Chicory, Grapefruit, and Manchego Salad (page 65).

Clams with Chorizo and Fennel

Serves 2 to 4

I didn't really eat clams until my twenties—they just weren't available in the Catskills in the nineties—and I've been trying to make up for it ever since. Clams have no shortage of virtues. They're relatively affordable compared to most seafood and cook in minutes, but what I really love is that they can take on nearly any flavor. Here, shallots and fennel cook along with chorizo until soft and aromatic, forming the base for an impossibly addictive broth. (If you don't eat meat, skip the chorizo and add an extra ½ teaspoon of crushed red pepper flakes so you don't miss out on the spice.)

Serving this with bread is completely optional, but it's great for sopping up all that broth.

INGREDIENTS

2 pounds Littleneck clams
1 tablespoon olive oil
½ pound chorizo (about 2 links), casings removed, crumbled
1 medium shallot, roughly chopped
1 medium fennel bulb, roughly chopped
2 large garlic cloves, minced
½ teaspoon crushed red pepper flakes
1 teaspoon kosher salt
1 cup dry white wine, such as sauvignon blanc or pinot grigio
Juice of 1 lemon
2 tablespoons fennel fronds, roughly chopped
2 tablespoons cilantro, roughly chopped
Crusty bread, for serving

DIRECTIONS

One hour before cooking, check each clam. If any shells are open, lightly tap them on a counter. If the shells close, add them to a large bowl. If not, that clam has died and must be discarded. Fill the bowl with cold water. After 30 minutes, discard the water and refill with cold water once more to remove any grit. After 30 minutes more, scrub the clams to remove any excess grit on the outside of the shells, then return them to the bowl. Discard the water once again and refill with cold water until you're ready to cook the clams. This will ensure the clams stay as fresh as possible.

In a large pot over medium-high heat, add the olive oil and chorizo and cook, stirring occasionally, until browned and crispy, 5 to 7 minutes. Remove the chorizo with a slotted spoon and transfer to a paper towel–lined plate, leaving the fat in the pot.

Add the shallot and fennel and cook, stirring occasionally, until softened, for 5 to 6 minutes.

Add the garlic, red pepper flakes, and salt and cook, stirring often, until the garlic is fragrant, about 1 minute.

Add the cooked chorizo and cleaned clams to the pot and stir to combine.

Add the wine and place a lid on the pot. Cook until the clams have opened, 7 to 8 minutes. Discard any clams that haven't opened.

Remove the pot from the heat and add the lemon juice, fennel fronds, and cilantro, and stir to combine. I like serving clams with crusty bread. Brush a slice of bread with olive oil and rub with a garlic clove and place under the broiler for a minute or two, just until it becomes golden brown. The clams are best served immediately, but can be stored in a sealed container in the refrigerator for up to 2 days.

Save the fennel stalks and fronds for the Snap Pea, Daikon, and Fennel Slaw (page 77).

Curried Mussels with Basil

Serves 2 to 4

Similar to clams, mussels are an affordable, sustainable seafood option that works with multiple flavor combinations and cooks in minutes. This recipe is vaguely inspired by mussels I've eaten in Thai restaurants, but uses Indian curry powder (rather than red or green curry paste), since that's often what I have on hand. I use a blend of coconut milk, white wine, and lime juice for the base that gets spiked with garlic, ginger, and chilies. This recipe can be easily doubled if you're looking to feed a group.

INGREDIENTS

2 pounds mussels
2 tablespoons olive oil
1 large shallot, thinly sliced
3 garlic cloves, minced
1-inch knob ginger, minced
1 Fresno chili, thinly sliced
1½ tablespoons curry powder
1½ teaspoons kosher salt
1 cup dry white wine, such as sauvignon blanc or pinot grigio
1 can (13.5 ounces) unsweetened full-fat coconut milk
Zest and juice of 1 lime
1 cup basil leaves
Crusty bread, toasted, to serve

DIRECTIONS

One hour before cooking, check each mussel. If any shells are open, lightly tap them on a counter. If the shells close, add them to a large bowl. If not, that mussel has died and must be discarded. Fill the bowl with cold water. After 30 minutes, discard the water and refill with cold water once more to remove any grit. After 30 minutes more, scrub the mussels to remove any excess grit or barnacles on the outside of the shells, then return to the bowl. Discard the water once again and refill with cold water until you're ready to cook the mussels. This will ensure the mussels stay as fresh as possible.

Heat the olive oil in a large pot over medium-high heat. Once the oil begins to shimmer, add the shallot and cook until golden brown, about 4 minutes. Add the garlic, ginger, and chili and cook until softened and fragrant, 1 to 2 minutes. Add the curry powder and salt and cook until well combined, about 30 seconds.

Add the wine and cook, scraping up any brown bits on the bottom of the pot, until the smell of alcohol burns off, about 2 minutes. Add the coconut milk and mussels and place the lid on the pot. Cook until the mussels have opened, discarding any that don't, 4 to 5 minutes.

Stir in the lime zest and juice and basil. I like serving mussels, like clams, with crusty bread. Brush a slice of bread with olive oil and rub with a garlic clove and place under the broiler for a minute or two, just until it becomes golden brown. The mussels are best served immediately, but can be stored in a sealed container in the refrigerator for up to 2 days.

With your jar of curry powder, make the Curry Butter Popcorn (page 45). Use up the rest of the basil bunch with the Chilled Green Soup (page 97) or Orecchiette with Carrot Top Pesto and Peas (page 113). Use up ginger with the Olive Oil–Fried Egg with Chili Crisp (page 219), Farro with Mushrooms (page 123), Whole Red Snapper with Cilantro and Lime (page 169), or Stone Fruit Crisp (page 179).

Whole Red Snapper with Cilantro and Lime

Serves 2 to 4

I know a whole fish can seem intimidating, but as long as you ask your fishmonger to descale and gut it (and you should), I promise this recipe for red snapper could not be easier.

Other whole fish to consider are trout, branzino, bass, and mackerel. The size of the fish will alter the cooking time, but just keep in mind you want to cook it just until it flakes easily when nudged with a fork. I love this zippy rub of garlic, ginger, jalapeño, and lime, and it will work on all of these fish. But you can't go wrong with any combination of aromatics: citrus, tender herbs, and any allium will impart flavor.

INGREDIENTS

2 tablespoons olive oil, plus more for greasing

2 large garlic cloves, grated

1-inch knob ginger, grated

2 limes, 1 zested and thinly sliced, 1 cut into wedges, divided

1 jalapeño, seeded if desired, minced

½ bunch cilantro, finely chopped

3 teaspoons kosher salt

1 red snapper (about 3 pounds), descaled and fins removed

DIRECTIONS

Preheat the oven to 425°F. Lightly grease a rimmed baking sheet with olive oil.

In a medium bowl, combine the olive oil, garlic, ginger, lime zest, jalapeño, cilantro, and salt.

On a cutting board, pat the fish dry all over with paper towels, including the cavity. Make three incisions on the bias on each side of the fish, making sure to cut through the skin.

Rub the snapper all over, including the cavity, with the cilantro mixture. Place the lime slices inside the cavity.

Transfer the snapper to the prepared baking sheet. Bake until the fish is just cooked through and easily flakes when nudged with a fork, 25 to 30 minutes, depending on the size of your snapper.

Using a knife, scrape the skin back from the flesh of the fish. Carefully remove the top fillet and transfer to a serving platter. Pick up the tail and remove the spine of the fish with the pin bones (they should easily peel off in one motion). Transfer the second fillet to the serving platter.

Serve the snapper with the lime wedges. The snapper can be stored in a sealed container in the refrigerator for up to 3 days.

Save cilantro for the California Citrus Salad (page 55), Carrot Ribbon Salad (page 59), or Baja-Style Fish Tacos (page 171). Use up ginger with the Olive Oil–Fried Egg with Chili Crisp (page 219), Farro with Mushrooms (page 123), Curried Mussels with Basil (page 166), or Stone Fruit Crisp (page 179). If you have a garden or even a few potted plants, save the bones of the snapper and bury them in the soil. They make great fertilizer.

Baja-Style Fish Tacos

Serves 4

While there's some debate about who created the fish taco, most food historians and writers agree that they became popular in Baja California, Mexico, during the 1950s. Light, crispy battered fish is topped with thinly sliced cabbage, pico, and doused in crema. They're best eaten immediately while they're still piping hot from the fryer.

INGREDIENTS

Pico de Gallo

2 cups cherry tomatoes, quartered

½ medium red onion, roughly chopped

1 medium jalapeño, finely chopped

½ cup cilantro leaves, roughly chopped

¾ teaspoon kosher salt

Juice of 1 lime

Tacos

4 cod fillets, cut into 2-inch pieces

2 teaspoons kosher salt

1 teaspoon freshly ground black pepper, plus more to taste

1½ cups all-purpose flour

1 tablespoon paprika

¼ teaspoon cayenne pepper

¾ teaspoon baking powder

1 egg, beaten

1 can (12 ounces) club soda

Oil, such as canola or vegetable, for frying

8 corn tortillas, lightly toasted, to serve

1 small cabbage, thinly sliced, to serve

Crema or sour cream, to serve

2 limes, quartered, to serve

DIRECTIONS

Make the pico de gallo: In a medium bowl, add the tomatoes, onion, jalapeño, and cilantro, and stir to combine. Right before serving, add the salt and lime juice and stir to combine.

Make the tacos: Pat the cod dry with paper towels. Season with salt and black pepper on both sides.

In a large bowl, add the flour, salt, black pepper, paprika, cayenne, and baking powder, and whisk to combine. Add the egg and beat until just combined. The batter will be lumpy. Add the club soda and whisk until the batter is smooth, with no more lumps.

Dip each piece of cod into the batter to fully coat, shaking off any excess, then transfer to a plate while the oil heats up.

Add 4 inches of oil to a large pot over high heat and bring to 350°F on a digital thermometer.

Working in batches, carefully lower the battered cod into the oil and fry until the batter is puffed and golden brown, 3 to 4 minutes. Transfer the fried cod to a wire rack over a rimmed baking sheet or paper towel–lined plate to drain any excess oil. Season with more salt to taste.

Serve the fish in tortillas topped with pico de gallo, cabbage, crema, and lime wedges. The fish tacos are best served immediately, as they'll start to lose their crispiness if they remain at room temperature for too long.

Use any leftover cabbage to make the Sausage and DIY Kraut (page 145). Fry corn tortillas for the Ceviche Tostada (page 173). Use the other half of the red onion for the Pork Shoulder Larb (page 151), Ceviche Tostada (page 173), or the Tuna and White Bean Salad (page 175). Cilantro is added to the California Citrus Salad (page 55), Carrot Ribbon Salad (page 59), Charred Cauliflower with Zhoug and Pine Nuts (page 93), or Whole Red Snapper with Cilantro and Lime (page 169).

Ceviche Tostada

Serves 2 to 4

I think it's a requirement for anyone visiting Los Angeles to go to Mariscos Jalisco, an Eastside food truck serving an assortment of Mexican-style seafood dishes. One of my favorite dishes they serve is a tostada piled high with ceviche, a seafood medley spiked with lime juice. The crispy tortilla balances the acidity from the fish, while also holding the whole thing together.

Ceviche has long been a part of the culinary makeup of South America, with origins dating back hundreds of years in Peru. These days ceviche is served all over Latin America, each country offering a slightly different version. In Peru, corn and sweet potatoes are often tossed into ceviche; in Ecuador there's ketchup; in Chile grapefruit juice is added in addition to lime; and in Panama lemon juice is used. Jalapeño, red onion, and avocado remind me of the version served at Mariscos Jalisco, but you could also add tomatoes, coconut flakes, mango, or corn.

It's key to use the freshest seafood possible here. Talk to your fishmonger to see what came in that day. You could use shrimp, scallops, red snapper, sea bass, flounder, grouper, and even salmon. Whatever fish you choose, the preparation is the same. The acid from the lime juice "cooks" the fish, breaking down the protein until it becomes opaque, which is why here you let it sit in the marinade. Be forewarned that anything over an hour can result in a tough, rubbery fish.

INGREDIENTS

1 pound firm whitefish, such as rockfish, wahoo, bass, or grouper, cut into bite-size pieces
Zest of 2 limes
Juice of 6 limes
½ red onion, thinly sliced
1 jalapeño, thinly sliced
1½ teaspoons kosher salt, plus more for the tostadas
3 tablespoons vegetable oil
8 corn tortillas
1 avocado, roughly chopped
1 bunch cilantro, leaves and stems finely chopped

DIRECTIONS

Add the fish, lime zest and juice, onion, jalapeño, and salt to a large bowl and mix to combine. Make sure the fish is submerged in the lime juice. If not, juice another lime and add that to the bowl, too. Cover the bowl with plastic wrap and refrigerate until the fish is opaque and just "cooked" through, 40 to 45 minutes.

While the fish is marinating, make the tostadas. Heat the vegetable oil in a large pan over medium high. Once the oil begins to shimmer, add a tortilla and cook until golden brown. Flip the tortilla with tongs and continue cooking until golden brown and crispy, 1 minute more. Transfer the tostada to a paper towel–lined baking dish and sprinkle with salt. Repeat with the remaining tortillas. The tostadas can be made up to 24 hours in advance and kept in a sealed container at room temperature.

Add the avocado and cilantro to the bowl with the marinating fish and stir until just combined. Immediately serve the ceviche piled high on the crispy tortillas.

Leftover tortillas can be served with the Baja-Style Fish Tacos (page 171). Use the other half of the red onion for the Pork Shoulder Larb (page 151), Crispy Sweet Potato Skins with Crème Fraîche (page 47), or California Citrus Salad (page 55).

Tuna and White Bean Salad

Serves 2 to 4

Bright and crunchy, this tuna salad is light enough that you don't need a midday nap later, and substantial enough to keep you full until dinner. The best part is that it takes minutes to throw together and lasts up to three days in the fridge.

INGREDIENTS

½ red onion, thinly sliced

1 garlic clove, grated

2 tablespoons olive oil

¼ teaspoon kosher salt

½ teaspoon freshly ground black pepper

Zest and juice of 1 lemon

2 celery stalks, thinly sliced

1 can (15 ounces) white beans, drained and rinsed

1 can (5 ounces) olive oil–packed tuna

3 tablespoons parsley leaves and stems, roughly chopped

DIRECTIONS

Add the onion, garlic, olive oil, salt, and pepper to a large bowl and marinate for 10 minutes. Add the lemon zest and juice, celery, beans, tuna, and parsley, and stir to combine. Serve as is, or piled on toast. The tuna and white bean salad can be stored in a sealed container in the refrigerator for up to 3 days.

Leftover celery stalks can be used up in the Celery Salad with Walnuts and Pecorino (page 63), Root Vegetable Pot Pie (page 88), or Corn Soup with Garlic Chips (page 99). Save parsley for the Spicy Brothy Bacony Beans (page 115), Lentil Soup with Parsley (page 117), Farro with Mushrooms (page 123), Crispy Chicken Thighs with Chickpeas and Olives (page 133), Herby Chicken Salad (page 134), or Red Wine Braised Short Rib Ragout (page 137).

DESSERTS

Stone Fruit Crisp

Buttermilk Shortcakes with Roasted Strawberries

Whole Wheat Chocolate Chunk Cookies

Banana Tarte Tatin

Orange Meringue Semifreddo

Candied Citrus Peels

Brown Butter Apple Cake

One-Bowl Fudgy Brownies

Salted Maple Vanilla Bean Pot de Crème

Baklava

Marbled Sour Cream Coffee Cake

Ice Cream Sundae

Any Fruit Granita

Buttermilk Shortcakes with Roasted Strawberries

Serves 6

When I was a kid, every year my dad would haul a strawberry shortcake from an Italian bakery in the East Village up to our house in the Catskills for my birthday. It was two layers of a yellow cake, topped with a thick layer of whipped cream, and studded with thickly sliced strawberries. As an adult, I love the nostalgia of that cake, but my tastes have changed. These days, I want my desserts to be a little less sweet, and these shortcakes are exactly what I want. You could leave the strawberries raw, but roasting them concentrates the flavor while simultaneously creating a syrup to spoon over a cloud of whipped cream and a tender shortcake.

If you don't have buttermilk on hand, you can easily make a swap. Add one cup of whole milk to a bowl along with the juice of one lemon and let it stand at room temperature for about five minutes, or until the milk starts to curdle and the surface looks chunky.

INGREDIENTS

Roasted Strawberries

6 cups (3 pints) strawberries, stems removed, large ones halved, small ones kept intact

3 tablespoons granulated sugar

¼ teaspoon kosher salt

1 vanilla bean pod, seeds scraped, or 1 teaspoon pure vanilla extract

Peels from 1 lemon

2 tablespoons water

Shortcakes

2 cups all-purpose flour, plus more for dusting

¼ cup granulated sugar

1 teaspoon baking powder

1 teaspoon kosher salt

½ cup (1 stick) unsalted butter, frozen

1 cup plus 1 tablespoon buttermilk, cold, divided

1 tablespoon turbinado sugar

DIRECTIONS

Preheat the oven to 375°F.

Make the roasted strawberries: Add the strawberries, sugar, salt, vanilla bean pod and seeds, lemon peels, and water to a 9-inch square baking dish. Roast until the strawberries are softened and have released their juices, about 30 minutes. Reserve the strawberries and their juices in a sealed container until ready to use. The strawberries can be roasted ahead and stored in the refrigerator for up to 3 days.

Make the shortcakes: Increase the oven temperature to 425°F. Line a baking sheet with parchment paper.

In a large bowl, whisk the flour, granulated sugar, baking powder, and salt.

Using a cheese grater, grate the cold butter into the flour mixture. Working quickly, use your hands to toss the butter in the flour.

Pour 1 cup of buttermilk into the flour mixture and use a rubber spatula to stir into a shaggy dough. The dough will be very sticky at this point.

Turn the dough out onto a generously floured surface. If the dough looks too sticky, dust with a bit more flour. Form the dough into a 6×8-inch rectangle, and sprinkle with more flour.

Continued on next page

Whipped Cream

1 cup heavy cream

3 tablespoons powdered
   sugar

Divide the dough into three equal parts and stack on top of each other. Turn the dough 90 degrees, then use your hands to press down into a 6×8-inch rectangle.

Cut the dough into six equal squares and transfer to the prepared baking sheet.

Brush the biscuits with the 1 tablespoon of buttermilk and sprinkle with the turbinado sugar.

Bake the biscuits for 20 to 25 minutes, until the tops are golden brown. They can be stored in a sealed container at room temperature for up to 2 days.

Make the whipped cream: Add the cream to a medium bowl and use an electric hand mixer on medium-high speed to whip until soft peaks form, 2 to 3 minutes. Add the powdered sugar and beat just until combined, about 1 minute. If you want to make whipped cream by hand, follow the same process but use a whisk instead of a mixer. This will require patience, some arm strength, and a bit more time. The whipped cream can be stored in a sealed container in the refrigerator for up to 3 days. Before serving, whisk the whipped cream once more to bring it back to life.

Slice the shortcakes in half and add a spoonful of the roasted strawberries and a large dollop of whipped cream to one side. Place the other half on top and serve immediately.

Use up the rest of your buttermilk with the BLT Salad (page 57), or the Buttermilk Ricotta with Honey and Toasted Macadamia Nuts (page 30). Save the vanilla bean pod to make your own extract (page 241). Extra heavy cream can be used for the Root Vegetable Pot Pie (page 88), Creamy Preserved Lemon Pasta (page 109), Banana Tarte Tatin (page 187), Orange Meringue Semifreddo (page 189), or Ice Cream Sundae (page 203).

Whole Wheat Chocolate Chunk Cookies

Makes about 30 cookies

I'm not a huge chocolate person (I know, I know), so of all the cookies, chocolate chip has never been my favorite. I set out to make a version to change my own mind, and in the process of testing these—no lie, thirty times—they became my favorite cookie. The secret here is slowly melting butter until it transforms from sunny yellow to golden brown. The brown butter adds an almost toffeelike flavor, while whole wheat flour adds a nuttiness, creating a cookie with layers of flavors. (If you don't have whole wheat flour, all-purpose will work.) I also took a cue from cookie expert Sarah Keiffer, who's known for her famous pan-banging cookies. This recipe uses more of a tap than a bang, but the principle is the same: the cookies become crispy on the outside, and chewy on the inside.

I love using chocolate wafers, or feves, rather than chips, which melt better when baked. Chocolate wafers can be found at specialty grocery stores or ordered online. Chocolate chips or a chopped bar of chocolate work, too; just make sure it's high-quality chocolate, since you'll really be able to taste the difference here. My go-to brand is Guittard.

INGREDIENTS

1 cup (2 sticks) unsalted butter
2¼ cups whole wheat flour
½ teaspoon baking soda
1½ teaspoons kosher salt
1 cup granulated sugar
1 cup light brown sugar, packed
2 eggs plus 1 egg yolk, at room temperature
1 teaspoon pure vanilla extract
1½ cups semisweet chocolate wafers
Flaky sea salt, to finish

DIRECTIONS

Add the butter to a small saucepan over medium-high heat, twirling the pan occasionally until the butter melts and becomes foamy. Reduce the heat to low and continue cooking for about 3 minutes, or until the butter is golden brown and smells nutty. Remove the pan from the heat and cool for at least 5 minutes before using.

In a medium bowl, add the flour, baking soda, and salt, and whisk to combine.

In a large bowl, add the melted butter, granulated sugar, and brown sugar, and whisk to combine until smooth. Add the eggs and egg yolk, one at a time, mixing until just combined. Add the vanilla and mix until combined.

Add the dry ingredients and use a rubber spatula to fold until just combined, with no visible streaks of flour. Add the chocolate wafers and fold until just combined.

Cover the dough and refrigerate for at least 1 hour, or up to 24 hours, which helps intensify the flavor of the cookies. Meanwhile, arrange an oven rack in the upper third position.

Preheat the oven to 350°F. Line two large rimmed baking sheets with parchment paper.

Continued on next page

Roll the dough into 1½-inch balls and place six on each prepared baking sheet, spacing 3 inches apart. Bake one sheet at a time, until the edges are golden brown and the centers are slightly puffed, about 13 minutes. Tap the baking sheet on the counter to deflate the cookies.

Let cool for 5 minutes on the baking sheet and sprinkle with flaky sea salt. Transfer the cookies to a wire rack to finish cooling to room temperature. While the cookies are resting, bake the other sheet of cookies. Alternate baking sheets until all the dough is used.

The cookies keep in a sealed container at room temperature for up to 5 days.

Use that bag or bar of semisweet chocolate for the One-Bowl Fudgy Brownies (page 195). Save the leftover egg white for the Coconut Ginger Pecan Granola (page 209).

Banana Tarte Tatin

Serves 4 to 6

If you're tired of using up browning bananas with *another* banana bread, try this decadent banoffee pie–inspired tarte tatin instead. In this version, I make a quick caramel, which can be made ahead or even doubled and divided for a later use, to really capture that banoffee pie flavor. Tarte tatin is best eaten straightaway while the puff pastry is crisp and flaky, so plan accordingly.

INGREDIENTS

3½ tablespoons unsalted butter

¼ cup plus 2 tablespoons granulated sugar

1 tablespoon heavy cream

Pinch of kosher salt

2 to 3 ripe bananas, cut into ¼-inch slices

Flour, for dusting

1 sheet puff pastry, thawed

DIRECTIONS

Preheat the oven to 375°F.

Melt the butter in a medium cast iron or stainless steel pan over medium-high heat. Add the sugar and stir constantly until the caramel becomes smooth and golden brown, about 6 minutes. Some cues to keep in mind: After 3 minutes, the sugar will start to become smooth, but the butter will still be separated. After 5 minutes, the butter and sugar will combine and start to become smooth. Turn off the heat and add the heavy cream and salt and stir for about 1 minute more, or until completely smooth. Arrange the banana slices side by side, making sure they're touching but not overlapping, in the caramel until the surface is fully covered.

Lightly flour your work surface. Cut out a 10-inch circle from the puff pastry, using your pan as a stencil, with a paring knife. Reserve the scraps for a later use. Lightly flour the pastry and roll out into a 12-inch circle. Place the pastry into the pan, and with your fingers, crimp the excess pastry along the side to fit the diameter of the pan.

Bake until the pastry is puffed and golden brown, about 40 minutes.

Carefully take the pan out of the oven and place a cutting board or large plate over the pan. Quickly invert the pan onto the board or plate, using a pot holder and your fist to tap on the top of the pan to help release the tart. Lift the pan up slowly. If any banana slices stick to the caramel, transfer them back to the pastry. Let cool for 10 minutes, or until the caramel has set slightly. Serve immediately.

If you're looking for another way to use puff pastry, check out the Greens Skillet Pie (page 83). Save heavy cream for the Root Vegetable Pot Pie (page 88), Creamy Preserved Lemon Pasta (page 109), Buttermilk Shortcakes with Roasted Strawberries (page 181), Orange Meringue Semifreddo (page 189), or Ice Cream Sundae (page 203).

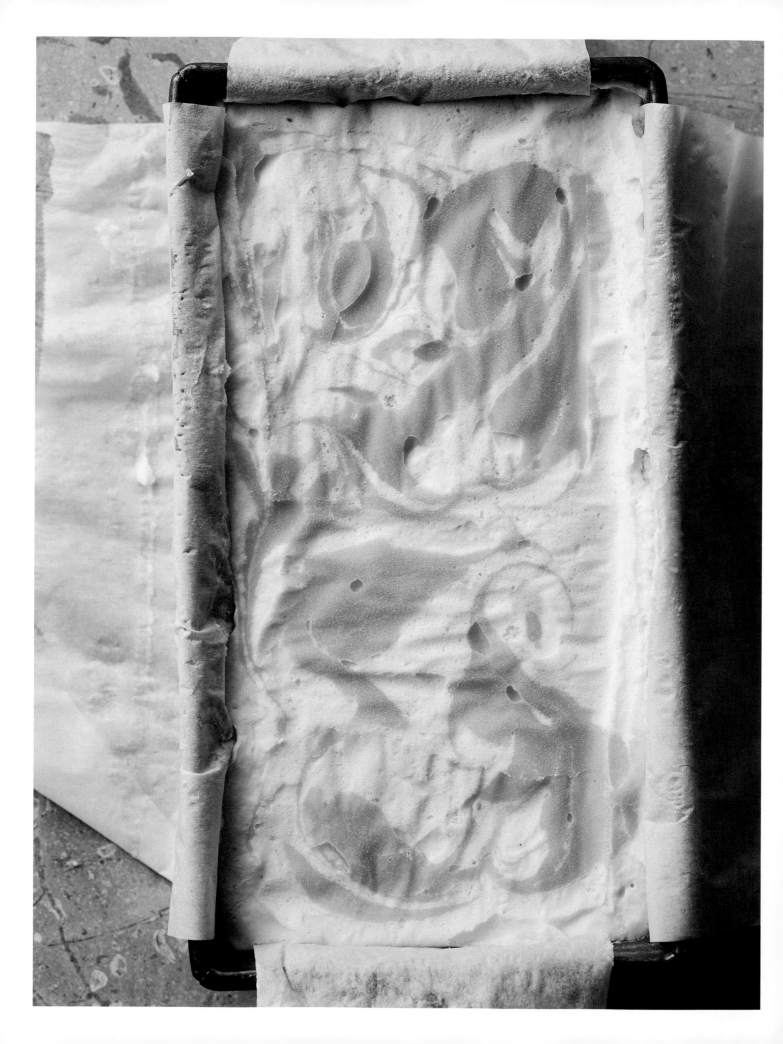

Candied Citrus Peels

Since citrus rinds can't be composted (they're too acidic for the delicate microorganisms in compost, which means your compost won't reach its full potential), make use of them with this recipe. Candied citrus peels are often eaten around the holidays, but can be made year-round. It may seem excessive to blanch the peels three times, but if you don't, they'll be too bitter to eat. Oranges are classic, but you can use any type of citrus you have on hand.

INGREDIENTS

Citrus of choice, such as oranges, grapefruit, lemons or limes

1¼ cups granulated sugar, divided

1 cup water

DIRECTIONS

On a cutting board, slice off the ends of the citrus creating two flat surfaces on either end. Place the citrus on one flat side onto the cutting board. Using a sharp chef's knife, carefully slice the rind of the citrus in a downward motion, leaving as much of the pith as you can on the fruit, until you have removed all of the rind. Reserve the peeled fruit for another use. Using a paring knife, carefully slice any part of the white pith off the rinds, then slice into ¼-inch slices.

Bring a small pot of water to a boil over high heat. Add the citrus peels and blanch for 10 minutes. Drain the peels and repeat the blanching process two more times.

Add the 1 cup of sugar and water to another small pot and bring to a boil over medium-high heat, whisking occasionally until the sugar is dissolved. Add the blanched citrus peels to the syrup. Reduce the heat and simmer until the peels are softened and flexible, 1 hour.

Transfer the peels to a wire rack set over a baking sheet to dry out until the texture is tacky rather than sticky, 1 to 2 hours.

Add the remaining ¼ cup of sugar to a bowl. Add the candied peels and toss until fully coated. The candied peels can also be left as is or dipped into melted chocolate. Store the candied peels in a sealable container at room temperature for up to 2 weeks.

Use the flesh of oranges and grapefruit for the California Citrus Salad (page 55). Grapefruit can be saved for the Chicory, Grapefruit, and Manchego Salad (page 65).

Brown Butter Apple Cake

Serves 6 to 8

There's an apple tree a few feet from the house where I grew up. Every fall my mom and I would look forward to picking its fruit. Then we'd go overboard making applesauce, using our neighbor's press for cider, and sticking apples in any dessert we could think of. This cake recipe would have been the perfect solution, as the batter is equal parts apple to filling. If you've got a lot of apples around—from an orchard or from the grocery store—here's what to make next.

The recipe calls for a nine-inch springform pan, but an eight- or ten-inch one will work as well; just be sure to adjust the baking time by a few minutes in either direction (eight-inch, less time; ten-inch, more).

INGREDIENTS

¾ cup (1½ sticks) unsalted butter, at room temperature, plus more for greasing

Zest and juice of 1 lemon, divided

3 medium baking apples, such as Granny Smith or Pink Lady

2 eggs

¾ cup granulated sugar

1 teaspoon pure vanilla extract

1 cup all-purpose flour

1 teaspoon baking powder

½ teaspoon kosher salt

¾ teaspoon ground cinnamon

¾ teaspoon ground cardamom

1 tablespoon turbinado sugar

1 tablespoon powdered sugar

DIRECTIONS

Preheat the oven to 350°F. Generously grease a 9-inch round springform pan with butter. Line the bottom of the pan with parchment paper.

Prepare a large bowl of cold water and add the lemon juice. Peel and dice the apples into ½-inch pieces and transfer to the bowl of water. This will prevent the apples from discoloring while you make the batter.

Add the butter to a small saucepan and melt over medium-high heat, swirling the pan occasionally until the butter becomes foamy. Reduce the heat to low and continue cooking until the butter is golden brown and smells nutty, about 3 minutes. Remove the pan from the heat and cool for at least 5 minutes before using.

In a large bowl, beat the eggs with a hand mixer. Add the granulated sugar and beat until light and fluffy. Add the browned butter, vanilla, and lemon zest, and beat until smooth. Alternatively, this can be done in a stand mixer or by hand.

Add the flour, baking powder, salt, cinnamon, and cardamom, and beat until just combined. Drain the apples in a colander then add them to the batter, using a rubber spatula to fold until just combined.

Transfer the batter to the prepared springform pan and smooth the top with a rubber spatula. Sprinkle the turbinado sugar over the cake. Bake until the top is golden brown, glossy, and cracked, about 40 minutes.

Cool for at least 30 minutes in the springform pan before unmolding. Remove the springform and transfer the cake to a serving platter. Place the powdered sugar in a fine-mesh sieve and dust the cake all over. The cake can be stored in a sealed container at room temperature for up to 3 days—just wait to add the powdered sugar until serving.

Any extra apples can be used to make the Fruit Shrub (page 241) or even the Any Fruit Granita (page 205).

One-Bowl Fudgy Brownies

Makes about 24 brownies

This recipe is based on a version my mom made from *Joy of Cooking*. She brought them to every potluck and school activity, and they were a hit every time. Whereas I find most brownies to be too cakey, this version is unbelievably fudgy and boasts a crinkly top, too. Two decades later, I still can't get enough. Plus, they're easy—these brownies are made in one bowl and bake in just under thirty minutes.

If you don't like or are allergic to walnuts, you can leave them out or use another type of nut, like hazelnuts, almonds, or cashews. I think they add great texture that shouldn't be missed.

INGREDIENTS

½ cup (1 stick) unsalted butter, melted, plus more for greasing
1½ cups semisweet chocolate
1½ cups granulated sugar
4 eggs
2 teaspoons pure vanilla extract
1 cup all-purpose flour
Pinch of kosher salt
¾ cup walnuts, roughly chopped, optional
Flaky sea salt

DIRECTIONS

Preheat the oven to 350°F.

Grease a 9×13-inch baking pan with butter. Line the pan with parchment paper.

Place the chocolate in a microwave-safe bowl and microwave in 30-second intervals, stirring after each, until the chocolate is melted.

In a large bowl, use a hand mixer to beat the melted chocolate and melted butter until combined. Add the sugar and beat until combined. Alternatively, this can be done in a stand mixer or by hand.

Add the eggs and vanilla and beat until combined.

Add the flour and the pinch of kosher salt, and carefully beat until just combined, making sure not to overbeat the batter.

Add the walnuts, if using, and fold in with a rubber spatula until just combined.

Pour the brownie batter into the prepared baking pan and smooth out the top with the rubber spatula.

Place the baking pan in the oven on the middle rack. Bake for about 25 minutes, or until the top is crinkly and a toothpick comes out clean.

Cool for 5 minutes at room temperature, then sprinkle with flaky sea salt. Cut the brownies into your size of choice (I like mine on the smaller side, about 1½-inch squares). The brownies can be stored in a sealed container at room temperature for up to 1 week.

Use leftover chocolate for the Whole Wheat Chocolate Chunk Cookies (page 185). Walnuts can be used in the Baklava (page 199), Celery Salad with Walnuts and Pecorino (page 63), White Wine Braised Leeks (page 75), or Hanger Steak with Walnut Romesco (page 143).

Salted Maple Vanilla Bean Pot de Crème

Serves 4

I was certainly not the first kid who grew up with long, dreary winters to try this, but when I was seven, it felt like a revelation. After a fresh snow, which in the Catskills happens weekly, if not daily, I would trudge outside and pack a bowlful of snow. Then I'd come inside and pour maple syrup over the top, letting it seep into the snow, making a kind of slushy maple candy. This pot de crème is a few tiers above my snow and syrup mixture, but still feels like a discovery.

INGREDIENTS

1¾ cups heavy cream
¾ cup whole milk
1 vanilla bean, seeds scraped, pod reserved or 1 teaspoon vanilla extract
6 egg yolks
2 tablespoons granulated sugar
⅛ teaspoon kosher salt
¼ cup pure maple syrup
Flaky sea salt, to serve

DIRECTIONS

Add the cream, milk, and vanilla bean seeds and scraped pod to a medium saucepan and set over medium heat. Cook, stirring often, until the mixture begins to simmer, about 6 minutes. Turn off the heat and steep for at least 1 hour at room temperature to infuse the cream.

Preheat the oven to 300°F. Bring a kettle filled with water to a boil.

Reheat the cream mixture over medium heat until simmering, about 5 minutes, then strain through a large fine-mesh sieve into a large glass measuring cup with a pour spout, discarding the vanilla bean pod.

In a large bowl, whisk the egg yolks, sugar, and salt until smooth. While still whisking, pour the cream mixture into the eggs and keep whisking until smooth. Once again, pour the mixture through the fine-mesh sieve into the measuring cup, then divide it among four 4-ounce ramekins or oven-safe bowls.

Place the ramekins in a 9-inch square pan or 9×13-inch baking dish and carefully fill the dish with boiling water from the kettle going halfway up the sides of the ramekins. Place a piece of aluminum foil securely over the baking dish and poke it with a fork all over to let some steam release while baking. Very carefully transfer the pan to the oven. Bake until the edges of the pot de crème are just set, and the center still has a slight jiggle, 25 to 30 minutes. They will continue to set as they chill.

Let the ramekins sit in the water for 10 minutes, then very carefully transfer to the counter to cool to room temperature, about 1 hour. Pour 1 tablespoon of maple syrup over each pot de crème, tilting the ramekin to cover the entire surface. Transfer the ramekins, uncovered, to the refrigerator to chill for at least 2 hours, and up to 2 days.

Before serving, sprinkle with flaky sea salt.

Use egg whites to make the Orange Meringue Semifreddo (page 189) or Coconut Ginger Pecan Granola (you can also use maple syrup here, page 209). If you have leftover heavy cream, use it for the Root Vegetable Pot Pie (page 88) or Banana Tarte Tatin (page 187).

Baklava

Makes 24 pieces

Baklava's origins lie in the Ottoman Empire, and this dessert can be found all over the Middle East today. There are dozens of varieties across the region; most include some form of pastry and nuts. I like the kind I ate in Turkish restaurants as kid, which used sheets of phyllo brushed in melted butter and spoonfuls of toasted mixed nuts. I use a traditional mix of walnuts and pistachios here, but you could use any assortment of nuts—almonds and hazelnuts would be delicious—and when I have half a bag of pine nuts around, I use those, too. The whole thing gets drenched in honey syrup infused with cinnamon and orange, which seeps into every layer.

INGREDIENTS

Syrup
1 cup granulated sugar
½ cup honey
1 cup water
1 cinnamon stick
2 orange peels

Baklava
2 cups whole walnuts
2 cups pistachios, shelled
1 teaspoon ground cinnamon
1 teaspoon ground cardamom
8 ounces frozen phyllo dough (1 roll, half of a 16-ounce package), thawed
1 cup (2 sticks) unsalted butter, melted

DIRECTIONS

Preheat the oven to 350°F.

Make the syrup: In a small pot, add the sugar, honey, water, cinnamon stick, and orange peels and bring to a boil over medium-high heat, stirring until the sugar dissolves. Once the mixture boils, reduce the heat and simmer for 20 minutes. Let cool to room temperature.

Make the baklava: In the bowl of a food processor, add the walnuts and pistachios and pulse until the nuts are finely ground with a few larger pieces. Alternatively, you can chop them by hand.

Transfer the nuts to a large bowl and add the cinnamon and cardamom and stir to combine.

Line a rimmed baking sheet with parchment paper.

Carefully place one sheet of phyllo on the parchment paper and brush with melted butter. Continue layering five sheets of phyllo, brushing each sheet with melted butter. Sprinkle ⅓ of the walnut and pistachio mixture over the phyllo dough. Continue layering with five layers of buttered phyllo sheets, ⅓ portion of nuts, five layers of phyllo, and the remaining nuts. The last layer should have six sheets of phyllo.

Using a sharp knife, cut the baklava into twelve 4-inch squares, then cut each square on the diagonal to create triangles, creating 24 pieces. Bake for about 50 minutes, or until the phyllo is golden brown and crispy. Remove the cinnamon stick and orange peels from the syrup. Pour the cooled syrup over the baklava as soon as it comes out of the oven, making sure to distribute it evenly. Let the baklava rest at room temperature for at least 1 hour before serving.

The baklava will last up to 1 week in a sealed container at room temperature.

Use the other roll of phyllo dough in the package for the Lamb Phyllo Pie (page 157). Don't let that orange go to waste! Slice it up for the California Citrus Salad (page 55) or make Candied Citrus Peels (page 191).

Marbled Sour Cream Coffee Cake

Serves 9

My boyfriend went on about his great Aunt Carlita's sour cream coffee cake for a year before I finally got to try it. And he was right: it was well worth the hype. Carlita's version was moist, light, and airy. Soon I was craving it as much as he was, and between visits to his family, I worked on my own version. I made a few tweaks, like cutting down the sugar (again, I like my desserts less sweet). I also split the batter in two, boosting each respective bowl with vanilla extract and cocoa powder. The batters get layered together to create a marbled effect, which satisfies both vanilla and chocolate lovers alike, then topped with a crunchy streusel topping, which is good enough to eat on its own.

INGREDIENTS

Topping
½ cup light brown sugar, packed
¼ cup all-purpose flour
1 ½ teaspoons ground cinnamon
¼ teaspoon kosher salt
½ cup (1 stick) unsalted butter, cold and cubed, divided

Cake
1 ¾ cups all-purpose flour, sifted
1 ¼ teaspoons baking powder
¼ teaspoon kosher salt
1 cup (2 sticks) unsalted butter, at room temperature
1 ¼ cups granulated sugar
2 eggs
1 cup sour cream
2 teaspoons pure vanilla extract
2 tablespoons cocoa powder

DIRECTIONS

Preheat the oven to 350°F. Grease a 9×5-inch loaf pan with ½ tablespoon of butter.

Make the topping: In a medium bowl, add the brown sugar, flour, cinnamon, and salt, and stir to combine. Add the remaining butter and use your fingers to work it into the dough until the butter is the size of lima beans. Uneven butter pieces are okay—they add great texture to the topping.

Make the cake: In a medium bowl, add the flour, baking powder, and salt, and whisk to combine.

In a large bowl, add the butter and sugar and beat with a hand mixer until pale yellow and fluffy, about 2 minutes. Add the eggs one at a time and beat until just combined, scraping the bowl down after each addition. Add the sour cream and beat to combine, scraping the bowl down again.

Add the dry ingredients to the wet ingredients and beat until just combined. Spoon half the batter into another bowl—I add it back to the bowl that held dry ingredients to avoid washing another dish. To one bowl, add the vanilla and beat to combine. To the second bowl, add the cocoa powder and beat until just combined.

Alternate adding heaping spoonfuls of the vanilla batter and chocolate batter to the prepared pan, which will create a marbled effect. Smooth the top with the back of a spoon to create an even layer, and sprinkle the topping over it.

Bake until the topping has hardened and created a crackly layer over the cake and when a toothpick inserted into the middle comes out clean, about 50 minutes. Let the cake cool completely before serving. Slice into your desired size squares (I like 3-inch squares).

The coffee cake dries out quickly, so make sure to store it in a sealable container as soon as it's cool. Stays fresh for up to 3 days in a sealable container at room temperature.

Cocoa powder is key for the hot fudge sauce—another of my boyfriend's family recipes!—to make an Ice Cream Sundae (page 203). Use up the rest of that sour cream in the Tomato and Caramelized Onion Galette (page 69); Snap Pea, Daikon, and Fennel Slaw (page 77); or the Fingerling Potato and Leek Top Frittata (page 215).

Ice Cream Sundae

I'll take an ice cream sundae over almost any dessert. Here I've traded in maraschinos for cherries spiced with anise and bay leaves and cooked until jammy, chopped peanuts for toasted slivered almonds, and homemade hot fudge sauce. I think this trio works particularly well together, but you could get creative with other toppings like the roasted strawberries (page 181) or the caramel sauce from the Banana Tarte Tatin (page 187). That's the joy of an ice cream sundae: you can really make it your own.

INGREDIENTS

Hot Fudge Sauce
¾ cup granulated sugar
3 tablespoons cocoa powder
¼ teaspoon kosher salt
2 tablespoons water
½ cup heavy cream
2 tablespoons unsalted butter
1 teaspoon pure vanilla extract

Spiced Poached Cherries
1 cup granulated sugar
2 cups water
1 cinnamon stick
1 star anise
1 bay leaf
¼ teaspoon kosher salt
½ teaspoon black peppercorns
3 orange peels
1 pound (about 3 cups) cherries, pitted, fresh or frozen and thawed

Toasted Almonds
½ cup sliced almonds

Ice cream of choice, for serving

DIRECTIONS

Make the hot fudge sauce: Add the sugar, cocoa, and salt to a medium saucepan over medium heat and stir to combine. Add the water and stir until the cocoa dissolves, about 30 seconds. Add the cream, whisking often, until the mixture begins to boil. Continue stirring until the sauce begins to just thicken, 3 to 4 minutes. Remove the pan from the heat and add the butter and vanilla and stir to combine. The fudge sauce can be eaten right away, or cooled to room temperature, transferred to a sealed container, and stored in the refrigerator for up to 1 week.

Make the poached cherries: Add the sugar, water, cinnamon stick, star anise, bay leaf, salt, peppercorns, and orange peels to a medium saucepan over medium-high heat, and stir to combine. Continue to whisk until the sugar dissolves. Add the cherries and simmer over medium-high heat until softened, 45 to 50 minutes. Remove the pan from the heat and let cool to room temperature. The cherries can be served immediately or transferred to a sealed container and stored in the refrigerator for up to 1 month.

Make the toasted almonds: Heat a pan over medium-high heat. Once the pan feels warm, add the almonds and cook, stirring occasionally, until lightly browned and toasted, 2 to 3 minutes. The almonds can be stored in a sealed container at room temperature for up to 1 week.

Serve ice cream of choice topped with the fudge sauce, spiced cherries, and toasted almonds.

Use any leftover cherries for the Stone Fruit Crisp (page 179) or make the Fruit Shrub (page 241). Almonds can be swapped in for walnuts in the Hanger Steak with Walnut Romesco (page 143), Baklava (page 199), or topped on the Farro Porridge (page 213). Cocoa is used in the Marbled Sour Cream Coffee Cake (page 200). Save heavy cream for the Root Vegetable Pot Pie (page 88), Creamy Preserved Lemon Pasta (page 109), Buttermilk Shortcakes with Roasted Strawberries (page 181), Banana Tarte Tatin (page 187), or Orange Meringue Semifreddo (page 189).

Any Fruit Granita

Serves 6 to 8

Granita sounds a lot fancier than it is. It's kind of like a snow cone that takes minutes to make. You blend your fruit of choice with sugar, transfer it to the freezer, and scrape it up to get that slushy texture. This recipe works best with berries and grapes (my favorite), or a combination of the two, although you can also try it with other fruit.

INGREDIENTS

2 cups fruit of choice, thawed
   if frozen
½ cup boiling water
Juice of 1 lemon
⅓ cup granulated sugar
⅛ teaspoon kosher salt

DIRECTIONS

In the bowl of a food processor, add the fruit, hot water, lemon juice, sugar, and salt, and blend to combine.

Transfer the fruit mixture to a 9-inch square pan and freeze for 45 minutes.

Take a fork and rake the granita back and forth to break up the mixture. The mixture will be very slushy. Freeze the granita until completely frozen, at least 4 hours.

Before serving, use a fork to scrape up the granita and serve immediately. The granita can be covered and stored in the freezer for up to 2 weeks.

This is How You Make a Cheese Plate (page 27) is a great way to use leftover fruit. If you used grapes and have leftovers, try the Mustardy Pork Tenderloin with Grapes and Red Onion (page 149).

BREAKFAST

Coconut Ginger Pecan Granola

Blueberry Dutch Baby

Farro Porridge

Fingerling Potato and Leek Top Frittata

Saucy Tomatoes and Eggs

Olive Oil–Fried Egg with Chili Crisp

Cauliflower and Cheddar Strata

Coconut Ginger Pecan Granola

Makes 6 cups

Homemade granola always packs more flavor, and it's generally more affordable, so I buy granola ingredients in bulk and store them together in a drawer since they last forever, then I'm always able to make a batch. While I think the combination below is hard to beat—coconut flakes and candied ginger taste downright tropical—you can use whatever nuts or fruit you have on hand. Just make sure to keep the proportions of three cups of oats to three cups of add-ins for a well-balanced mix. Other nuts like walnuts, pistachios, cashews, or almonds work, along with dried fruit, seeds, dark chocolate, and even candied pineapple. One thing you can't swap in is quick-cooking oats. They're precooked and thinner than rolled oats, and won't work in this preparation.

INGREDIENTS

3 cups rolled oats
1 cup pecans, chopped
1 cup candied ginger, chopped
1 cup large unsweetened coconut flakes
1 teaspoon ground cardamom
½ teaspoon ground cinnamon
1 teaspoon kosher salt
½ cup olive oil
½ cup pure maple syrup
2 egg whites

DIRECTIONS

Preheat the oven to 300°F. Line a rimmed baking sheet with parchment paper.

In a large bowl, mix the oats, pecans, ginger, coconut flakes, cardamom, cinnamon, and salt until combined.

In a glass measuring cup, add the olive oil and maple syrup and whisk to combine.

Pour the syrup mixture over the oat mixture, and mix to combine. Add the egg whites and mix to combine, then spread the mixture out in an even layer on the baking sheet.

Bake until golden brown and fragrant, about 50 minutes, mixing halfway through with a wooden spoon.

Cool to room temperature. Store in an airtight container for up to 3 weeks.

Use up egg yolks for the Aioli (page 23), Celery Salad with Walnuts and Pecorino (page 63), or Blistered Asparagus and Peas with Salt-Cured Egg Yolks (page 73). Maple syrup can be used on the Salted Maple Vanilla Bean Pot de Crème (page 197). Pecans are fantastic in the Sweet and Salty Nut Mix (page 43).

Blueberry Dutch Baby

Serves 2 to 4

I love pancakes, but I hate standing over the stove flipping them. When I'm short on time, but still want that pancake vibe, I make a Dutch baby. Mix up a quick batter with eggs, flour, and milk, pour that into a hot pan, and bake until golden brown and fluffy. It tastes like a pancake—maybe better—and there's no flipping required.

My favorite fact about Dutch babies is that they're not really Dutch. The name comes from a German family in Seattle who ran Manaca's Cafe. The story goes that the owner's daughter couldn't pronounce the name of this dish in German, and so it became the Dutch baby.

Room-temperature eggs and milk are crucial for the success of a Dutch baby. If the ingredients are too cold, they won't allow the Dutch baby to rise properly (science). If you're in a rush, microwave cold milk or heat it on the stove until just warm to the touch. Cold eggs can be put in a bowl with warm water and they'll be ready to use in five minutes.

INGREDIENTS

3 eggs, at room temperature
1 teaspoon pure vanilla
  extract
Zest of 1 lemon
½ cup all-purpose flour
2 tablespoons granulated
  sugar
¼ teaspoon kosher salt
½ cup whole milk, at room
  temperature
2 tablespoons unsalted butter
1 cup (½ pint) blueberries,
  fresh or frozen and thawed
Powdered sugar, to serve

DIRECTIONS

Preheat the oven to 425°F.

In a large bowl, beat the eggs with the vanilla and lemon zest until well combined.

Add the flour, granulated sugar, and salt, and whisk until the batter is smooth. Slowly add the milk, whisking until well combined. There should be no lumps.

Heat the butter in a medium cast iron or stainless steel pan over medium-high heat. Once the butter melts, about 2 minutes, add the batter. Sprinkle the blueberries over the top of the batter and immediately transfer the pan to the oven.

Bake until the Dutch baby is golden brown and puffed, 18 to 20 minutes.

Place the powdered sugar in a fine mesh sieve and tap over the Dutch baby to sprinkle in an even layer. Serve immediately, as the Dutch baby will collapse by the minute.

Save blueberries for the Any Fruit Granita (page 205) or the Fruit Shrub (page 241).

Farro Porridge

Serves 4

Farro has a similar chew to steel-cut oats but has a nuttier flavor. I reach for it when I want something warm and filling, but a little different in the morning. Add fresh fruit, poppy seeds, and nuts for a sweet option, or make it more savory with leftover roasted vegetables and Parmesan sprinkled on top.

INGREDIENTS

1¼ cups farro
¼ cup unsalted butter
2¼ cups whole milk or
  alternative milk of choice
½ teaspoon kosher salt
Toppings of choice

DIRECTIONS

Place the farro in the bowl of a food processor and pulse until the farro is partially ground to the size of cornmeal, with some bigger pieces still visible.

In a small pan, melt the butter over medium-high heat. Once the butter is melted, add the ground farro and stir until coated with butter and lightly golden, about 1 minute.

Slowly pour in the milk, whisking to prevent any clumps. Add the salt and continue to stir until the mixture begins to boil.

Reduce the heat to low and continue to stir often until the mixture is thickened and most of the milk is evaporated, 10 to 12 minutes. For an even thicker porridge, continue cooking until your desired consistency. Remove the porridge from the heat and let cool for 5 minutes.

Divide among four bowls and serve immediately with toppings of choice, such as crème fraîche or sour cream, fruit, toasted nuts, or even the Spiced Poached Cherries (page 203).

Make the Farro with Mushrooms (page 123) with leftover farro. Any leftover fresh fruit can be turned into the Any Fruit Granita (page 205), or used for the Fruit Shrub (page 241).

Fingerling Potato and Leek Top Frittata

Serves 4

Every home cook should know how to make a frittata. It's one of those standby breakfasts that tastes great with nearly any leftover vegetable or protein. Make it for brunch with friends, or if you're the type to meal-plan, bake it on Sunday and you can eat a slice for breakfast every day of the week. The combination of leek tops, thinly sliced buttery potatoes, and sour cream reminds me of sour cream and onion chips.

This recipe specifies that you should use leek tops—that means the dark green part of the plant. I wrote it because it's something you'd usually toss. Leek tops are perfectly edible and have more subtle flavor than the white and light green parts of the leek, and I wanted to celebrate them.

INGREDIENTS

1 tablespoon olive oil

½ pound fingerling or Yukon Gold potatoes, thinly sliced into ⅛-inch slices

2 tablespoons unsalted butter

2 cups (4 to 5 leeks) thinly sliced leek tops, dark green parts

1¼ teaspoons kosher salt, divided

1 teaspoon freshly ground black pepper, divided

6 eggs

¼ cup sour cream

DIRECTIONS

Preheat the oven to 350°F.

In a medium cast iron or stainless steel pan, heat the olive oil over medium-high heat. Once the oil begins to shimmer, add the potatoes and cook for about 5 minutes, stirring occasionally, or until the potatoes are easily pierced with a knife and golden brown on the edges.

Add the butter to the same pan. Once the butter melts, add the leeks and cook, stirring occasionally, until the leeks have wilted and turned a darker green, 2 to 3 minutes. Season with 1 teaspoon of salt and ½ teaspoon of pepper and stir to combine. Remove the pan from the heat.

In a large bowl, add the eggs and sour cream and whisk until the mixture is smooth with no lumps. Add the remaining ¼ teaspoon of salt and ½ teaspoon of pepper, along with the reserved potato and leek mixture. Pour the mixture back into the same pan, and bake until the frittata is just set and browned on top, 25 to 30 minutes.

Let the frittata cool for 5 minutes before serving. The frittata lasts for up to 4 days in a sealed container in the refrigerator.

Use the white and light green parts of leeks for the White Wine Braised Leeks (page 75) or the Charred Corn with Burrata (page 79). Extra fingerlings can be turned into the Smashed Potato Salad (page 81) or served along with the Aioli (page 23). Save sour cream for the Marbled Sour Cream Coffee Cake (page 200), Tomato and Caramelized Onion Galette (page 69), or Snap Pea, Daikon, and Fennel Slaw (page 77).

Saucy Tomatoes and Eggs

Serves 4

Whenever I make this tomato sauce, I double the batch. I use it for Eggplant Parmesan (page 85) and stir it into pasta, and any leftovers I keep on hand ready for this baked egg dish for breakfast. It's like the Italian version of shakshuka. The sauce is on the chunky side, which is how I like it.

INGREDIENTS

1 tablespoon olive oil

2 tablespoons unsalted butter

1 yellow onion, finely chopped

3 garlic cloves, minced

¼ cup tomato paste

½ teaspoon crushed red pepper flakes

1½ teaspoons kosher salt

½ teaspoon freshly ground black pepper

1 can (28 ounces) whole tomatoes

1 sprig basil, plus leaves, torn, to serve

4 ounces goat cheese, crumbled

4 eggs

Toast, to serve

DIRECTIONS

In a large Dutch oven, heat the olive oil and butter over medium heat. Once the butter is melted, reduce the heat to medium-low and add the onion and cook for about 30 minutes, or until the onion is softened and golden. Add the garlic and stir for about 3 minutes, or until fragrant. Increase the heat to medium-high, add the tomato paste, and stir until the paste begins to turn brick red and caramelize, about 3 minutes.

Add the red pepper flakes, salt, and black pepper, and stir to combine. Add the tomatoes, breaking them up with your hands. Pour in the tomato juice from the can. Add the basil. Bring to a boil, then reduce the heat and simmer for 30 minutes. Let cool to room temperature, then remove the basil. The tomato sauce can be stored in a sealed container in the refrigerator for up to 5 days, or frozen for up to 3 months.

When you're ready to make breakfast, add the tomato sauce to a medium skillet. Stir in the goat cheese. Make four indentations in the sauce with the back of a spoon. Crack the eggs into the sauce, one in each indentation. Set the heat to medium-low and simmer until the egg whites are just set and the yolks reach your desired consistency, 20 to 25 minutes. Serve immediately with toast.

Olive Oil–Fried Egg with Chili Crisp

Makes 2½ cups Chili Crisp

While there are so many fantastic chili crisp brands out there (a favorite is the Sichuan-inspired version Fly By Jing makes), if you're ever running low, and you need a spoonful, I want you to know that you probably have all the ingredients to make your own version at home. While this addictive condiment adds great heat to anything you put on it, I love it with eggs. And a trick here from my mom: if you add an egg to a cold pan and let it slowly heat up over medium heat, the egg will be cooked perfectly every time. I also baste eggs with olive oil for crispy, almost paper-thin edges and runny yolks.

INGREDIENTS

Chili Crisp
2 cups vegetable oil
2 dried red chilies
10 garlic cloves, thinly sliced
1-inch knob ginger, julienned
3 large shallots, thinly sliced
1 cinnamon stick
3 star anise pods
¼ cup crushed red pepper
  flakes
1 tablespoon soy sauce
1 teaspoon granulated sugar
2 teaspoons kosher salt

Olive Oil–Fried Egg
1 tablespoon olive oil
1 egg
Toast, to serve

DIRECTIONS

Make the chili crisp: Add the vegetable oil, chilies, garlic, ginger, shallots, cinnamon stick, and star anise to a small pot over medium heat and cook until the oil begins to simmer. Reduce the heat to medium-low and simmer until the shallots become golden brown and crispy, 25 to 30 minutes. Remove the pot from the heat and let cool for 5 minutes.

While the aromatics are simmering in the vegetable oil mixture, add the red pepper flakes, soy sauce, sugar, and the salt to a small bowl and stir to combine.

Strain the vegetable oil mixture through a large fine-mesh sieve into the bowl with the red pepper flakes mixture. Discard the cinnamon stick, star anise, and red chilies, and transfer the garlic, ginger, and shallots to a paper towel–lined plate to dry out for 1 hour. This will help make the aromatics even more crunchy.

Stir the aromatics back into the oil and transfer to an airtight container. Makes 2 cups. The chili crisp can be stored in the refrigerator for up to 1 month.

Make the fried egg: Add the olive oil to a medium pan over medium heat. Immediately crack the egg into the pan while the pan is still cool. As soon as the whites begin to set, use a spoon to scoop up the olive oil in the pan and pour it over the egg whites. Cook until the yolks are set to your desired consistency and the edges are crispy.

Serve the egg on top of the toast with lots of chili crisp spooned over.

Use up ginger with the Farro with Mushrooms (page 123), Whole Red Snapper with Cilantro and Lime (page 169), Curried Mussels with Basil (page 166), or Stone Fruit Crisp (page 179). Extra dried red chilies can be used up in the Lamb Phyllo Pie (page 157).

Cauliflower and Cheddar Strata

Serves 6

Of all the breakfast recipes here, this strata might be my favorite. You can mostly make it ahead, it feeds a crowd, and the variations are endless—I end up tossing a lot of leftovers into this recipe, to delicious effect. This version is studded with roasted cauliflower, shallots, and cheddar cheese.

I make the cauliflower ahead and grate the cheese so this can be done in the least amount of time as possible, and I'd recommend you do the same. I love this combination, but the real joy of a strata is that you can use nearly any fillings like broccoli, spinach, kale, tomatoes, bacon, sausage, ham, and any kind of melty cheese.

INGREDIENTS

1 tablespoon unsalted butter

1 head cauliflower, florets removed and stem thinly sliced

¼ cup olive oil

1 teaspoon kosher salt, plus more to season

1 teaspoon freshly ground black pepper, plus more to season

9 large eggs

2¾ cups whole milk

2 heaping tablespoons Dijon mustard

8 ounces cheddar cheese, grated (about 2 cups)

2 large shallots, thinly sliced

8 cups sourdough bread, roughly torn cubes (from 1 large loaf; if it's going stale, even better)

2 tablespoons finely chopped chives

DIRECTIONS

Preheat the oven to 400°F. Grease a 9×13-inch baking dish with the butter.

Place the cauliflower florets on a baking sheet and drizzle with the olive oil, using your hands to coat each floret completely. Roast until charred on one side, about 25 minutes. Use a spatula to flip the cauliflower and continue roasting until the cauliflower is easily pierced with a knife and charred all over, about 10 minutes. Season the cauliflower with salt and pepper. The cauliflower can be made up to 3 days in advance and kept in a sealed container in the refrigerator.

Reduce the oven to 350°F.

In a large bowl, whisk the eggs, milk, Dijon, the 1 teaspoon of salt, and the 1 teaspoon of pepper. Add the cauliflower, cheddar, and shallots, and stir to combine. Add the bread and stir until fully coated. Gently pour the mixture into the prepared baking dish and transfer to the fridge to chill for 1 to 2 hours—any longer and the strata gets mushy. If you're short on time, you can go ahead and bake right away, but the chilling helps keep the strata custardy.

Bake until the custard is set and the bread is golden brown and crispy where it peeks out, about 45 minutes. Serve topped with the chives. The strata can be stored in a sealed container in the refrigerator for up to 2 days.

Leftover bread can be used in the Panzanella with Tomatoes, Melon, and Pickled Mustard Seeds (page 51); BLT Salad (page 57) to make Homemade Bread Crumbs (page 239); or sliced and served with Clams with Chorizo and Fennel (page 165); or Curried Mussels with Basil (page 166). Save chives for the Yogurt Chive Flatbread (page 37), Crispy Sweet Potato Skins with Crème Fraîche (page 47), Green Goddess Salad (page 53), or the Smashed Potato Salad (page 81).

TO THE LAST BITE: STOCKS, QUICK PICKLES, SYRUPS, AND MORE!

Preserved Lemons

Quick Pickled Vegetables

Homemade Stock

Homemade Bread Crumbs

Fruit Shrub

Syrups

Vanilla Extract

These recipes are the backbone of this cookbook–recipes that ensure as little goes to waste as possible. I always have a rotating selection of stocks, quick pickles, and syrups floating around my fridge. They add a boost of flavor without much effort. And they're a great way to use up scraps. Homemade chicken stock transforms farro into something extra savory; quick pickled red onions topping a fried egg adds a kick of acidity; and a splash of shrub in soda water makes me feel like I'm on vacation. What I love about these recipes is the flexibility and versatility—you can use them as a blueprint to start, and experiment from there depending on what you have in your fridge.

Preserved Lemons

Preserved lemons can be found in cuisines all over the world, from Northern Africa to India, and across the Middle East. There's good reason so many cultures practice this method of preservation—packing lemons in salt is a great way to extend the citrus season throughout the year. Chopped, sliced, or blended, they add intense lemon flavor, without any of the bitterness, and can brighten everything from grains to vinaigrettes and sauces.

The process of making preserved lemons could not be easier, though it does take some time. All you need is a handful of lemons and kosher salt. The salt both cures and preserves the lemons, so don't skimp on it. This same method can be used with Meyer lemons, limes, kumquats, and grapefruit, and the proportions can easily be multiplied, based on what and how much citrus you have on hand.

INGREDIENTS
2 medium lemons, scrubbed and dried
¼ cup kosher salt
¼ teaspoon black peppercorns, optional
¼ teaspoon coriander seeds, optional
1 dried bay leaf, optional

DIRECTIONS
On a cutting board, slice lemons lengthwise, making sure to leave them intact at the bottom.

Transfer the lemons to a small bowl with the salt. Use your hands to cover the lemons with the salt, inside and out. Some salt will fall to the bottom of the bowl, but do your best to scoop it up and cover the lemons well.

In a clean 5-ounce jar, add a handful of salt from the bottom of the bowl. Add a lemon and use a wooden spoon to roughly push it down, squeezing out most of the juice. Add another layer of salt from the bowl and repeat with the other lemon. Add the peppercorns, coriander seeds, and bay leaf, if using, making sure the lemon is submerged in the salt mixture.

Screw on the top of the jar loosely and set on your countertop for 3 to 4 weeks. Once you open the jar, transfer the lemons to the refrigerator. Preserved lemons last for up to 1 year refrigerated.

Use preserved lemons in the Israeli Couscous with Herbs (page 125) or the Creamy Preserved Lemon Pasta (page 109).

Quick Pickled Vegetables

Quick pickling simply means adding vegetables to a brine and storing them in the refrigerator, no canning required! You can quick pickle nearly any vegetable, making it an ideal way to use up anything you've got lingering in the crisper. Got half a red onion left over? Pickle it. Want to save those rainbow Swiss chard stems? Pickle 'em. Bought too many green beans at the market? Pickle them, too. You get the point.

A brine is made from a few ingredients: vinegar, water, salt, and sugar. The standard ratio is one to one for vinegar and water. But you can experiment with the salt and sugar proportions, and more. If you want a punchier pickle, add more salt. If you're looking for something more mellow, add a bit more sugar. You can also try out different types of vinegar depending on what flavor you're after. White distilled vinegar will provide a neutral flavor, while apple cider vinegar will impart a fruity one. Not only is quick pickling a great way to use up produce, but you can use the herbs and spices you have on hand to infuse the brine to make things a bit more interesting. I've listed a few places to start on the following pages.

Quick Pickled Red Onions

INGREDIENTS

½ cup apple cider vinegar

½ cup water

1 tablespoon granulated sugar

2 teaspoons kosher salt

1 teaspoon black peppercorns

1 teaspoon coriander seeds

1 bay leaf

1 red onion, thinly sliced

DIRECTIONS

Add the vinegar, water, sugar, salt, peppercorns, coriander seeds, and bay leaf to a small pot. Set over high heat and bring to a boil, whisking until the sugar and salt dissolve. Add the onion to the pot and remove from the heat. Cool at room temperature for 1 hour. Transfer the liquid and onion to a sealed container and store in the refrigerator for up to 1 week.

Quick Pickled Cucumbers

INGREDIENTS

½ cup rice vinegar

½ cup water

3 tablespoons granulated sugar

2 teaspoons kosher salt

2 garlic cloves

½ teaspoon crushed red pepper flakes

½ English cucumber, thinly sliced

DIRECTIONS

Add the vinegar, water, sugar, salt, garlic, and red pepper flakes to a small pot. Set over high heat and bring to a boil, whisking until the sugar and salt dissolve. Add the cucumber to the pot and remove from the heat. Cool at room temperature for 1 hour. Transfer the liquid and cucumber to a sealed container and store in the refrigerator for up to 1 week.

Quick Pickled Carrots and Radishes

INGREDIENTS

1 cup distilled white vinegar

1 cup water

3 tablespoons granulated sugar

3 teaspoons kosher salt

1 small shallot, thinly sliced

3 sprigs dill

3 medium carrots, peeled into ribbons with a vegetable peeler

3 radishes, thinly sliced

DIRECTIONS

Add the vinegar, water, sugar, salt, shallot, and dill to a small pot. Set over high heat and bring to a boil, whisking until the sugar and salt dissolve. Add the carrots and radishes to the pot and remove from the heat. Cool at room temperature for 1 hour. Transfer the vegetables and liquid to a sealed container and store in the refrigerator for up to 1 week.

Try your hand at pickling with the Mashed Sweet Potatoes with Honey Butter and Pickled Chilies (page 92).

Homemade Stock

I get such satisfaction from transforming leftovers into something entirely new. Stock is a great example. From the bones of a chicken or a few corncobs comes liquid gold that you can use over and over again. Precision doesn't matter here, and I often throw whatever scraps I have on hand into a pot and simmer until the stock takes on a golden hue. But I did write recipes here for you to get started. Over time, I hope you'll adjust these to your own preferences, more salt, less spice, or perhaps even more aromatics.

Measure then freeze stock in labeled containers so you know exactly how much is in it before you defrost. Add stock to White Wine Braised Leeks (page 75), Root Vegetable Pot Pie (page 88), Corn Soup with Garlic Chips (page 99), Spicy Brothy Bacony Beans (page 115), Lentil Soup with Parsley (page 117), Weeknight Rice (page 118), Farro with Mushrooms (page 123), Creamy Gruyère Polenta (page 119), Crispy Chicken Thighs with Chickpeas and Olives (page 133), Red Wine Braised Short Rib Ragout (page 137), or Pork Shoulder Larb (page 151).

Chicken Stock

Makes 8 cups

Chicken stock can be made with a chicken carcass, as written here, or at least a pound of leftover bones from the wings and thighs. Remember, the more bones you add, the more flavorful your stock will be. You can also make a vegetable stock by leaving the chicken out and following this same method.

INGREDIENTS

2 tablespoons olive oil
1 yellow onion, halved
4 medium carrots, roughly chopped
4 celery stalks, roughly chopped
4 garlic cloves, lightly smashed
4 sprigs parsley
4 sprigs thyme
2 teaspoons kosher salt
1 teaspoon black peppercorns
1 chicken carcass
1 Parmesan rind, optional
1 bay leaf
3 quarts water

DIRECTIONS

Add the olive oil to a large pot or Dutch oven over medium-high heat. Once the oil begins to shimmer, add the onion, carrots, and celery, and cook for about 15 minutes, stirring occasionally, or until the vegetables are lightly browned on all sides.

Add the garlic, parsley, thyme, salt, and peppercorns, and cook for about 2 minutes, or until the herbs and garlic are fragrant.

Add the chicken carcass, Parmesan rind, if using, the bay leaf, and water, and bring to a boil. Once boiling, reduce the heat to medium-low and simmer uncovered for about 2 hours, or until the liquid is reduced by one-third, occasionally skimming the fat off the top with a spoon.

Place a large fine-mesh sieve lined with cheesecloth or two paper towels over a large bowl and strain the stock, discarding the solids. Let the stock cool to room temperature before using.

The stock keeps in a sealed container in the refrigerator for up to 1 week, or frozen for 3 months.

Corn Stock

Makes 6 cups

There's no better way to capture the taste of summer than by making corn stock. If you've prepared a dish that only calls for kernels, like the Charred Corn and Burrata (page 79), and have a few cobs leftover, pull out your stockpot. Freeze corn stock for when corn is long out of season and you're counting the days to warmer months. Swap corn stock instead of chicken stock for a creamy risotto, use it to simmer dried beans, or save it for a summery soup, like the Corn Soup with Garlic Chips (page 99).

INGREDIENTS

2 tablespoons olive oil

1 yellow onion, halved

3 garlic cloves, lightly smashed

1 teaspoon black peppercorns

1 teaspoon coriander seeds

6 corn cobs, kernels removed

2 quarts cold water

1 dried bay leaf

1 Parmesan rind

DIRECTIONS

Heat the olive oil in a Dutch oven or large pot over medium-high heat. Once the oil begins to shimmer, add the onion cut-side down and cook, without moving, until charred, about 5 minutes.

Add the garlic, peppercorns, and coriander seeds, and cook until the garlic is golden brown, about 1 minute. Add the corn cobs, water, bay leaf, and Parmesan rind, and bring to a boil. Reduce the heat and simmer until slightly reduced, about 1½ hours.

Place a large fine-mesh sieve lined with cheesecloth or two paper towels over a large bowl and strain the stock, discarding the solids. Let the stock cool to room temperature before using.

The stock keeps in a sealed container in the refrigerator for up to 1 week, or frozen for 3 months.

Shrimp Stock

Makes 8 cups

If you're making a dish with shrimp, like the Poached Shrimp with Thousand Island Dressing (page 25), don't throw out the shells. I like to save the shrimp shells in a freezer bag until I'm ready to use them. They take up little freezer space, and you won't have to worry about that funky shrimp smell overtaking your refrigerator.

INGREDIENTS

2 tablespoons olive oil
1 yellow onion, halved
2 garlic cloves, lightly smashed
1 dried bay leaf
3 teaspoons kosher salt
1 teaspoon black peppercorns
4 cups shrimp shells, from about 3 pounds of shrimp
1 lemon, halved
5 sprigs parsley
2 quarts cold water

DIRECTIONS

Add the olive oil to a large stockpot or Dutch oven over medium-high heat. Once the oil begins to shimmer, add the onion, cut-side down, and cook without stirring until charred, 3 to 4 minutes.

Add the garlic, bay leaf, salt, and peppercorns, and stir until the garlic is fragrant, about 1 minute.

Add the shrimp shells and cook, stirring occasionally, until the shells turn pink, about 3 minutes.

Add the lemon, parsley, and water, and bring to a boil. Reduce the heat and simmer until reduced by one-fourth, about 30 minutes.

Place a large fine-mesh sieve lined with cheesecloth or two paper towels over a large bowl and strain the stock, discarding the solids. Let the stock cool to room temperature before using.

The stock keeps fresh in a sealed container in the refrigerator for up to 1 week, or frozen for 3 months.

Parmesan Broth

Makes 4 cups

If you've never had Parmesan broth, now's the time. It's subtle, but carries an umami flavor to anything you add it to, like Weeknight Rice (page 118) or the Spicy Brothy Bacony Beans (page 115). I keep Parm rinds in a bag in the cheese drawer until I've gathered enough to make this broth. It may take a few months to save enough rinds, but the final result is well worth the wait.

INGREDIENTS

8 ounces Parmesan rinds
2 teaspoons kosher salt
1 teaspoon black
   peppercorns
2 quarts cold water

DIRECTIONS

Add the Parmesan rinds, salt, peppercorns, and water to a large pot and set over medium-high heat. Once the water begins to boil, reduce the heat and simmer until the broth reduces by half and turns golden, stirring often to make sure the rinds don't stick to the bottom, about 1½ hours.

Place a large fine-mesh sieve lined with cheesecloth or two paper towels over a large bowl and strain the stock, discarding the solids. Let the stock cool to room temperature before using.

The stock keeps fresh in a sealed container in the refrigerator for up to 1 week, or frozen for 3 months.

Homemade Bread Crumbs

Makes 3 cups

I love the crispy, crunchy texture bread crumbs add to a dish, so I use them with abandon. Whenever I have a loaf of bread that's going stale, I make my own. On that note, it's best to use bread that's a few days old—a freshly baked loaf will become gummy when you pulse it in the food processor. Even if you make it through that stage, the bread crumbs won't dry out in the same way in the oven. I usually use sourdough, but pretty much any bread will work—brioche, focaccia, ciabatta, whole wheat, even hamburger buns! Once the bread is toasted, you can add any combinations of seasonings you like.

INGREDIENTS

6 cups roughly torn bread
(from 1 medium loaf)

DIRECTIONS

Preheat the oven to 300°F.

Place the torn bread on a baking sheet in a single layer and bake until the bread is lightly toasted, about 15 minutes. Flip the bread and continue baking until the bread feels dried to the touch, but hasn't yet browned, about 15 minutes more. Let the bread cool to room temperature.

Place the bread in the bowl of a food processor and pulse until you reach your desired consistency. I like uneven bread crumbs with a mix of smaller and bigger pieces. The bread crumbs stay fresh for up to a month in a sealed container at room temperature.

Use bread crumbs in the Chilled Green Soup (page 97) or Squash with Herby Salsa Verde (page 101).

Fruit Shrub

Makes 1 scant cup

Without fail, when it comes to fruit, I always buy more than I can actually eat. While fruit can be composted, when I've got a particularly gorgeous haul I really hate letting it go to waste. That's when I make a shrub. My fridge has an embarrassing amount of shrubs, made from peaches that started to bruise, blackberries that got too soft, and the last Sumo citrus of the season.

A shrub is a syrup made with fruit and vinegar. It can be drunk on its own, topped off with soda water, or mixed with ice and your booze of choice for a cocktail. There are two methods to making shrubs—cold press and hot press. I opted for the cold version since it takes even less time.

You can use just about any fruit here—berries, stone fruit, citrus, melon, even apples and pears. The type of vinegar is also up to you. I use apple cider vinegar for its naturally punchy, fruity flavor, but sherry, champagne, balsamic, and red wine vinegar work, too. You can also add other flavorings, such as herbs like basil or mint, ginger, or even whole spices like cardamom pods or star anise. Citrus zest works, too; just make sure it's organic to avoid ingesting any unnecessary pesticides.

INGREDIENTS
1 cup fruit of choice, roughly
   chopped
1 cup granulated sugar
½ cup vinegar of choice

DIRECTIONS
Add the fruit and sugar to a medium bowl and use a wooden spoon to mash until well combined. Cover the mixture with a kitchen towel and let rest on your countertop out of the sunlight for 24 hours. At this point, the fruit mixture should thicken and become syrupy—like the consistency of maple syrup.

Add the vinegar and stir to combine. Cover with a towel and let sit for another 24 hours to infuse the vinegar with the fruit mixture. Strain the liquid through a fine-mesh sieve into a sealable jar or container, discarding the fruit. Shrubs will last for up to 2 months in the refrigerator.

Syrups

Makes 1 cup

Infusing simple syrup couldn't be easier, and it's a great way to use up extra aromatics like herbs, ginger, rosemary, bay leaves, chilies, star anise, lavender, fennel, cardamom, and vanilla.

This version uses lemongrass, because I often have a few stalks around after I make the Pork Shoulder Larb (page 151). I use it for drinks—it's great with tequila and lime juice, and sometimes I just add a spoonful to soda water with a slice of cucumbers.

INGREDIENTS
1 cup water
1 cup granulated sugar
2 lemongrass stalks, white and light green parts roughly chopped

DIRECTIONS
Add the water, sugar, and lemongrass to a small pot over medium-high heat and bring to a boil, whisking occasionally until the sugar dissolves. Reduce the heat and simmer for 15 minutes. Strain the syrup through a large fine-mesh sieve into a sealable container or jar. Lemongrass syrup lasts for up to 1 month in a sealed container in the refrigerator.

Vanilla Extract

Makes 1 cup

It's shockingly easy to make your own vanilla extract, and it's the perfect way to use up leftover pods. I prefer to use vodka for its clean taste, but you can also use another spirit of choice—rum, bourbon, and brandy all work. Vanilla extract does take some time, but the final result is more flavorful, aromatic, and cheaper than the store-bought stuff.

INGREDIENTS

5 to 6 vanilla bean pods
1 cup 70 proof (or higher) vodka

DIRECTIONS

Add the vanilla bean pods to a clean, sealable jar or container. Cover the pods with the vodka, making sure they are fully submerged. Seal the jar and store in a cool, dark space for at least 6 months, and up to 1 year. Remove the vanilla bean pods and discard, and the vanilla extract is ready to use.

Use vanilla extract for the Stone Fruit Crisp (page 179), Whole Wheat Chocolate Chunk Cookies (page 185), Brown Butter Apple Cake (page 193), One-Bowl Fudgy Brownies (page 195), and Marbled Sour Cream Coffee Cake (page 200).

MENUS TO HELP YOU COOK (AND EAT!) TO THE LAST BITE

I make all the recipes in this book on a regular basis, but if you're wondering which go together especially well, I have a few ideas. Here are some menus, based on what's in season and who's coming to dinner. There are endless options, of course, but these are some of my favorite combinations.

SPRING DINNER

This menu celebrates the best of spring produce.

Aioli (page 23)

Blistered Asparagus and Peas with Salt-Cured Egg Yolks (page 73)

Smashed Potato Salad (page 81)

Spatchcock Paprika Chicken with Carrots and Onions (page 129)

Buttermilk Shortcakes with Roasted Strawberries (page 181)

SUMMER DINNER

This menu requires little stove time, and most of it can be made ahead, making it ideal for hot summer nights.

Poached Shrimp with Thousand Island Dressing (page 25)

Halibut with Tomatoes and Dill (page 161)

Charred Corn and Burrata (page 79)

Shaved Zucchini with Bagna Cauda (page 61)

Orange Meringue Semifreddo (page 189)

FALL DINNER

This menu is short, but hearty. The Eggplant Parmesan alone can more than fill you up, but I love serving a snack and a salad to round out the meal.

Crispy Sweet Potato Skins with Crème Fraîche (page 47)

Celery Salad with Walnuts and Pecorino (page 63)

Eggplant Parmesan (page 85)

Brown Butter Apple Cake (page 193)

WINTER DINNER

One of my favorite parts about winter is the excuse to spend all day in the kitchen. There's nothing more comforting to me than braising a big pot of short ribs on the stove.

Sweet and Salty Nut Mix (page 43)

Chicory, Grapefruit, and Manchego Salad (page 65)

White Wine Braised Leeks (page 75)

Creamy Gruyère Polenta (page 119)

Red Wine Braised Short Rib Ragout (page 137)

Salted Maple Vanilla Bean Pot de Crème (page 197)

VEGETARIAN DINNER

Many of the recipes in this book are vegetarian, but this menu highlights some of my favorites.

Whipped Feta and Charred Scallion Dip (page 35)

Yogurt Chive Flatbread (page 37)

Green Goddess Salad (page 53)

Tomato and Caramelized Onion Galette (page 69)

Stone Fruit Crisp (page 179)

VEGAN DINNER

More vegetarian recipes, but this menu has no dairy at all (and you won't miss it).

Corn Soup with Garlic Chips (page 99)

Marinated Red Peppers on Toast (page 29)

Carrot Ribbon Salad (page 59)

Charred Cauliflower with Zhoug and Pine Nuts (page 93)

Israeli Couscous with Herbs (page 125)

Any Fruit Granita (page 205)

GLUTEN-FREE DINNER

While it's no secret that I love all things gluten, there are plenty of (fantastic) recipes in this book that don't have any. This menu comes with lots of flavor, and no gluten in sight.

Curry Butter Popcorn (page 45)

California Citrus Salad (page 55)

Crispy Rice Salad (page 121)

Whole Red Snapper with Cilantro and Lime (page 169)

Ice Cream Sundae (page 203)

WEEKNIGHT DINNER

If you come over to my house on a weeknight, here's what I'm making. Everything comes together in less than thirty minutes.

Weeknight Rice (page 118)

Kale with Lemon and Parmesan (page 95)

Black Garlic Butter Salmon with Scallions (page 163)

SPECIAL OCCASION

Whether you're celebrating a birthday, promotion, anniversary, or just getting through another Monday, these dishes feel particularly fun and festive.

This is How You Make a Cheese Plate (page 27)

Farro with Mushrooms (page 123)

Roasted Radishes and Turnips with Brown Butter Caper Sauce (page 91)

Hanger Steak with Walnut Romesco (page 143)

Everyday Green Salad (page 57)

Salted Maple Vanilla Bean Pot de Crème (page 197)

ACKNOWLEDGMENTS

In the nearly three years of making this book, I've developed a deep appreciation for how many people it takes to not only put together a book, but to make it the best version possible. I'm sure everyone thinks their team is the best, but mine really is.

To Emily Graff, thank you for taking a chance on me. Your constant enthusiasm, support, hand-holding, weekly calls, and words of wisdom have made this book better. Even in the throes of edits, you made the whole process feel fun.

Thank you to the rest of the team at Simon & Schuster who worked tirelessly to create my dream book: Brittany Adames, Ruth Lee-Mui, Samantha Hoback, Natalia Olbinski, Jackie Seow, Alicia Brancato, Kimberly Goldstein, Rafael Taveras, Maxwell Smith, Irene Kheradi, Dana Canedy, Priscilla Painton, Stephen Bedford, Christine Calella, and Julia Prosser.

To my agent, Eve Attermann, thank you for championing my vision from day one. You and the rest of my team at WME (Adam Harris, Julia Bodner, Sam Birmingham, and Sian-Ashleigh Edwards) have been the best cheerleaders.

To Ilana Alperstein and Cassandra Chamoun, and the rest of the team at Mona Creative, thank you for rallying behind this book to get the word out in the most fun way possible.

To Nicole Franzen, thank you for bringing my vision to life. I've looked at these photos at least one thousand times and I still can't get enough of them. Rebekah Peppler, I don't know anyone else who would so readily fly halfway across the world in a global pandemic to be by my side. Thank you for sharing your talent, insights, humor, and, most of all, friendship with me. Karlee Rotoly, you make work feel like vacation. Cooking alongside you is easily one of my top ten favorite activities in life. Maeve Sheriden, even without being on set your presence was felt. Thank you for curating the most gorgeous selection of props I could have imagined.

To Ryan Nethery, my partner in life and love, thank you for your endless support in everything I do. Your discerning palate helped make these recipes the best they could be.

To Danielle Delott, not only were you the most thorough recipe tester, but your insights and opinions were truly invaluable. Thank you to my many friends who offered to test recipes, give notes, took my calls in hours of panic, and made edits— I couldn't have done it without you: Leah Wawro, Ryan Willison, Jenna Westover, Ann Fulton, Natalie Karic, Hannah Milligan, Jack Glasscott, Jamie Feldmar, Claire Gohorel, Colleen Clark, Grace Perry, Jesse Szewczyk, Samantha Sullivan, Ellee Durniak, Aishwarya Iyer, Robert Khederian, John Maher, Amanda Berrill, Hana Asbrink, Kort Havens, Erin Mosbaugh, Tania Metti, Olivia Gauthier, John Fulton, and Betsy Carter.

Thank you Wilson's Bread, Faiga Brussels at Good Cheap Food, Year & Day, East Fork Pottery, Hana Karim, Le Creuset, Tribe Alive, Flannery Beef, D'artagnan, and Murray's for all the contributions in food, clothes, and props, to make this book even more gorgeous. Thank you to Butch and David Wawro for opening up their home.

And of course, thank you to my mother, who inspired this book, hosted the two week photoshoot in her home (aka summer camp for adult women), and thinks everything I cook is the very best.

INDEX

ABOUT THE AUTHOR

ALEXIS DEBOSCHNEK is a cook, recipe developer, and video host based in the Catskills in upstate New York. She has developed recipes for Food52, The Kitchn, BuzzFeed Tasty, Chowhound, and Tasting Table, and hosts BuzzFeed Tasty's viral show *Chef Out of Water*. *To the Last Bite* is her first cookbook.